MW01119265

CATHOLIC

GUIDE

THROUGH

ANXIETY

2nd Edition
with revisions, updates, prayers,
quotes from the saints, and scriptural references

Catherine DiNuzzo, MA, LPC
with Meg Malone

Foreword by Fr. John Paul Mary Zeller, MFVA

"The more we learn about how beautifully and intentionally our brain and our body work together, the easier it is to see how we are lovingly and wonderfully made by God."

Catherine DiNuzzo

"The most efficacious way to have strong devotion to the
Sacred Heart of Jesus is through the Immaculate Heart of Mary."

- St. Margaret Mary Alacoque

TABLE OF CONTENTS

"The Sacred Heart is the symbol of that boundless love which moved The Word to take flesh, to institute the Holy Eucharist, to take our sins upon Himself, to offer Himself as a victim & sacrifice to the Eternal Father."

- St. Margaret Mary Alacoque

FOREWORD

FOREWORD

If only I would have known what I know now! How often have you said this throughout your life? You are unique.   You are unrepeatable.   You are a piece of work! I know I have heard the last one often!   I might change it to—you are a wondrous work in progress, created to give the world a glimmer of the brilliance of Almighty God!

Perhaps you do not think of yourself in this way.   Those of us who have struggled with some sort of mental health challenge most likely have not exactly glorified the greatness of the Lord in your infirmity.   We've questioned, "Why has God let this happen?" I'm willing to bet that most of you were scared to mention a mental health struggle, even to those closest to you, out of fear of being misunderstood or, worst of all, rejected.

In the Name of Jesus, who is Lord, may all those thoughts and considerations be banished from you. Our Lord knows your mind and your heart better than anyone on the face of the Earth. Our spiritual health is important. Our bodily health is important. Our mental health is important.   Have you ever considered that all three are tied together?

It seems that there has been so much written on striving for holiness of life, as well as how to maintain physical health, but when it comes to mental health, some people think and believe they are alone. This is not true! So many ordinary people at one point in their life have or do currently struggle with Anxiety.

Catherine DiNuzzo and Sacred Heart Mental Wellness desire to walk this journey with you - to give you the tools that you need to understand what exactly is happening in your body when anxiety enters the picture. You don't have to go through life in "survival mode," but you, by the Grace of God, combined with your cooperation and the love and care of others, can begin to THRIVE.

Be patient with yourself. God is patient with you. Give some deep thought and prayer into some of these principles and practices that Catherine recommends.

Even in your anxiety, Praise and Bless the Lord! It may be the furthest thing from your mind at the time, but the Psalms repeatedly remind us of the power of giving Praise to the Lord. I'd like to suggest some Psalms you might pray when you feel anxiety is getting the best of you: Psalm 23; 27; 34; 51; 61; 91; and 121.

Be assured of my prayers for you. You are not alone. When you bring your anxiety out into the Light, it has less power over you.

Sincerely in Christ,

Fr. John Paul

Father John Paul Mary Zeller, MFVA
Franciscan Missionaries of the Eternal Word, Irondale, AL

"Love overcomes,
love delights.
Those who love the
Sacred Heart rejoice."

- St. Bernadette

PREFACE

PREFACE

Good counselors must learn the process of self-disclosure early in their career. In short, self-disclosure is being comfortable with who you are and what you bring to each counseling situation. Here's a look at mine.

As a young child I was diagnosed with dyslexia and spent a lot of my school years learning how to overcome these challenges. My teachers always said I needed a different approach to reading and writing so my "high intelligence" wasn't hindered. Meanwhile, the devil told me the lie, *"you're not good enough."* The battle was waged for me to learn to know my intelligence, but I still found myself struggling to communicate it through reading and writing.

In this book you will hear a lot about how anxiety is based on the lie that you are not enough. Anxiety is such a big deal for me because I've lived it and I want you to overcome these lies in favor of the truth: you are loved, and you are good. Despite the dyslexia, I attended Emporia State University and the University of Colorado to graduate with my bachelor's degree in education, and my master's degree in counseling and human services.

This achievement taught me how to accept the challenges God allowed for me, to reject the lies of inadequacy, and find the tools needed to overcome the task at hand. Now I am a Licensed Professional Counselor (LPC) tasked with serving my clients and presenting the message of Sacred Heart Mental Wellness to those who need it. I've offered these concepts at large Catholic conferences, international parish missions, and to my clients in one-on-one counseling sessions.

The fruits of this growth are the lessons and skills learned along the way; this is the cornerstone of my apostolate Sacred Heart Mental Wellness. I created Sacred Heart Mental Wellness because I know and have seen how much God loves us, and I know how the world tells us something different.

"See what love the Father has given us, that we should be called children of God; and so we are. The reason why the world does not know us is that it did not know Him."
First Letter of St. John, Chapter 3, verse 1.

I refuse to let you go on believing the lies "I'm not enough" or "I'm unlovable." On the contrary... you ***ARE*** enough and you ***ARE*** lovable!

The mission of Sacred Heart Mental Wellness is to view mental health through a Catholic lens to proactively work with your mind, heart, and soul to guide you and convince you that you are loved.

"As the Father has loved me, so have I loved you; abide in my love." Gospel of St. John, Chapter 15, verse 9.

"Because your merciful love is better than life, my lips will praise you." Psalms, Chapter 63, verse 3.

The lies exist in the world, whether the Scriptures tell us something different or not. Another area the world lies to us and attempts to lead us astray is anxiety. A piece of this journey toward mental wellness will be learning the skills necessary for you to understand and overcome the feelings of anxiety.

Early in my career, I dreamed of writing a book. I knew He had given me a unique way of explaining things that were too good to keep to myself. He put the need to share mental wellness through His eyes on my heart. Every time I started to write, the lie *"you'll never be enough; a dyslexic can't write a book"* would creep into my mind. But that all changed one day in adoration. As I gazed upon the Blessed Sacrament, I heard God saying, "It's time, Catherine. I will give you everything you need to write this book. Trust in me."

And here we are, editing and republishing the second edition!

This is where my co-writer comes in. After that day, I read an amazing blog post by Meg Malone. As I read her writings, I heard her heart through the text. That's when I knew she was the one God sent to help me bring this book to life. We met to talk about this project, and I saw her ability to transform my thoughts, knowledge, and passion into a beautiful composition. She loves God and desires for others to know

Him. I feel like she was exactly the person God wanted to write this book with me.

As we start this journey together toward mental wellness, I want to use this space to show you that God knows our challenges and He loves us. The challenges that knock on your doorstep do not mean you've failed, or that you're not enough. It means that you need to act! You can take action by filling your tool belt with knowledge, understanding, and strategy. Then, you will be able to overcome the challenges that you face. I desire to guide you in fighting these challenges so you may relish in the good life God has given you!

Our aim is wellness. God desires this for you, as do I. This book will not only help you, but it will help you love those struggling alongside you. The better we understand the battle with anxiety, the bigger the victory we will celebrate.

"O give thanks to the Lord, for He is good; for His mercy endures forever!" First Chronicles, Chapter 16, verse 34.

"O Sacred Heart of Jesus,
fountain of eternal life,
Your Heart is a glowing
furnace of Love. You are
my refuge and my
sanctuary."

-St. Gertrude

INTRODUCTION

INTRODUCTION

"I'm not enough. I'll never be enough."

We've all been there. We've all thought it. It's a lie; he is a liar. Satan wants you to think that you're not enough so he can slither in and disturb your peace.

I've worked with the *"I'm not enough"* line of thinking my entire career. Folks believing that they're not enough is typically rooted in anxiety. I've given talks around the world on the topic of anxiety, its effects, and how to fight it. I've presented in conference rooms looking out at hundreds of faces, while each person sits there wondering, *"Am I crazy? I bet everyone can tell how nervous I am. Gosh, I shouldn't be sweating right now. I think I'm the only one in the room feeling this way!"*

It's so hard as a speaker to see the same, dire look in each person's eyes as if they were echoing one another's experience. It's not a you problem, it's an everyone problem. Everyone's face is communicating the same message: I'm not enough. Fearing your inadequacy, or believing this lie, is the kindling that fuels your feelings of anxiety.

After seeing this play out time and time again, I started looking into resources on anxiety. I found great books, classes, and tools, but I couldn't find the resource that told me exactly what happens in the brain when you feel anxious. My search to understand the biology of anxiety ended when I had the opportunity to work with military veterans with PTSD. Amid this work, I learned the biological causes of anxiety and how this information was a vital piece to understanding and overcoming the feelings of anxiety. Gaining a deeper understanding of the biological response led me to this conclusion. You're not crazy and your body is not bad.

Let's start at the beginning.

"God looked at everything He had made and found it very good." The Book of Genesis, Chapter 1, verse 31.

He's talking about you! God (the Father of All Good Things) created you to be enough. He created you whole. Hold onto this! Now stop to let the words soak in - from the moment of conception and by God's grace, you are, have been, and always will be enough because you are created by Love for Love. Your body is perfectly designed and doing exactly what it is created for.

No matter the age, culture, or gender, anxiety is a common struggle. You can be an amazing Catholic and struggle with anxiety! I've learned this firsthand. I've also learned the key that puts you in the driver's seat: understanding the biology of anxiety.

When you know what's going on in your head, you can work with it instead of against it. You will even praise God for giving you the survival mechanisms needed to stay safe. You will be able to intentionally practice and implement strategies that bring you back to the truth, to who you really are.

It may sound like a lot, but I promise, it's not scary. It's an act of love toward yourself, a choice toward peace. ***This book is not going to take away all of your anxiety, but it will empower you to manage it, and work with it.*** You will no longer be enslaved by your anxiety, but rather have power over it. This book will teach you how to cultivate mental wellness so you can live fully and wonderfully.

This material requires a few disclosures because anxiety and mental health are complicated topics. It's important to recognize that we are individuals who have unique experiences of anxiety, mental health, and medical care. This book does not aim to counsel individuals on their personal experience. It is not meant to replace therapy. Instead, the goal is to equip you with the necessary tools to effectively reduce your feelings of anxiety. I hope to show that you are not alone in this journey and offer a framework for building and sustaining mental wellness.

To get the most out of this book, I can't stress enough that you ought to start at the beginning and go cover to cover. Concepts in Chapter 1 will build the foundation to understand the brain's activity that causes the feelings of anxiety, which is incredibly important for overcoming it! If you skip forward, you will miss the prerequisites needed to successfully implement the given strategies and win the battle over your anxiety. I want to walk with you on this journey. So please, let's take it one step at a time. (We will go over the steps later in the book, but please trust me and trust the process.)

Next, the text often describes the limbic system as the animal brain and the frontal cortex as the thinking brain. These terms will be used interchangeably.

The goal of mental wellness is to proactively provide you the critical resources needed to prevent a mental health crisis. This book paired with the Sacred Heart Mental Wellness community is the easiest, fastest, cheapest, and most simplified way to help you build a strong mental health foundation.

AN EXPLANATION FROM SCRIPTURE

I think it is important to explain something early on in this book; the potentially confusing nature of the word "anxiety" found in Scripture. I am not a Scripture scholar, this is merely a quick explanation of a very complex situation. If this topic is of interest to you, please refer to the Church Fathers, as many have taken up this exercise at length.

Often, I come across folks who tell me all sorts of advice they've received or explanations that they've heard or read. Sometimes, the advice is poor and it is a detriment to good mental wellness. Frequently, people are told and believe that anxiety is sinful and that if a person were truly a 'good

Catholic' they would never experience anxiety. How are we to discern this conundrum?

We read *"Therefore I tell you, do not be anxious about your life."* (Matthew 6:25), and *"Have no anxiety about anything, but in everything by prayer and supplication with thanksgiving let your requests be made known to God."* (Philippians 4:6) Conversely, we hear the words of the Blessed Virgin Mary saying to her Son Jesus upon finding Him in the temple *"Behold, your father and I have been looking for you anxiously."* (Luke 2:48b) How is it that on the one hand we're told to have no anxiety, but St. Joseph and Mary (the Immaculate Conception herself) experienced anxiety?! Obviously, if Mary experienced anxiety then it cannot be sinful. And, Jesus would never lead His mother to sin nor into the near occasion of sin. So how do we understand this?

Much of the explanation comes from understanding first that the New Testament was not originally written in the English language and therefore we need to read the passages within the context they were written. (This goes for every verse in the Bible!) In Matthew 6 and Philippians 4 (verses above), anxiety is used to describe "a deep worry or concern" (the Greek word *merimnao*.) When we are advised against anxiety, we're being told essentially "do not have undue earthly worry about the problem at hand, but instead, give it over to God and allow Him to handle it. You are not in control, God is in control." When it comes to Luke 2 (as stated above) Joseph and Mary experience what St. Paul writes as a "deep sorrow or painful distress" (the Greek word *odynomenoi*.) One can imagine the feeling a parent goes through when their child is lost, and this is what they felt. The deep sorrow, the painful distress, the uneasiness, and the unknown ending to this situation. Joseph and Mary did not sin when they experienced odynomenoi. Joseph and Mary were experiencing the body's natural response to anxiety.

The word 'anxiety' is used numerous times in this book in the negative sense, and we typically mean (but not in every case) the form of merimnao - human worry or concern that we bring upon ourselves. This is when we are attempting to control the uncontrollable. However, the lines between merimnao and odynomenoi are often blurry. When we talk about anxiety and the possibility of overcoming anxiety, we are usually discussing it in the context of the body's natural response to outside factors, not something that is chosen or willed by the individual experiencing anxiety.

Ultimately, you must know that anxiety itself (and the biological response of the body) is not sinful. Sin is never involuntary, but rather, must be consented to with full knowledge, ie: an act of the will. As you read, know that anxiety (odynomenoi) is actually a God-given response and is for our good. Hopefully this becomes more clear as we move forward.

"Wherever a picture of
My Heart
is exposed and honored, it
will draw down all manner
of blessings."

-Jesus to St. Margaret Mary Alacoque

CHAPTER 1

MENTAL WELLNESS

CHAPTER 1 | MENTAL WELLNESS

Mental wellness is the ongoing process that aids your cognitive resilience, growth, and ability to flourish. Because I love analogies (you'll get to know this about me!), I am going to paint a picture of mental wellness that we will regularly circle back to throughout this book.

You have a sturdy house built on a strong, cement foundation. Your basement is stable due to the solid framework. The house is peaceful, clutter-free, and smells like homemade bread. The roof effectively keeps you protected from the elements, and the windows allow sunshine to flood in. Your mental wellness goal is this robust home.

HOLES AND SAND

Everyone desires a reliable home, a fortified domain where you can both take refuge and grow. We desire the same for our mental wellness, which is a good, natural desire. The problem is, we don't all have the perfect mental wellness. Why? No one has taught you, and that's okay. But you deserve to know how to cultivate a spectacular, robust, mental wellness. To get started, we need to begin at the root. It's just like when organizing your kitchen pantry, it's going to get messier before it gets better. So here it goes, let's recognize that everyone (even you) has a hole.

The hole, as you experience it, is not bad because it is often something that's happened outside of your control. However, this hole is something you don't like. It could be an experience, something you did or something that happened to you. It could be fears or insecurities. Whatever your hole might be, you associate that experience with danger. Your mind has created pathways that connect this experience to a threat. I will explain this process in depth later. But for now, I want you to remember we all have this hole. It does not mean you're a bad person. It means that you are human and need to learn the tools to build up from your hole.

PERSONAL HOLE EXAMPLE

When I was a young girl, I was swimming with my cousins. We were at the pool and one of my even younger cousins went below the surface and didn't come up for air. She stayed submerged. She went limp. I called for help, then dove toward her. I pulled her up and passed her onto adult care. She coughed up some water, and thankfully, was fine.

This situation was traumatic for me. I thought my cousin was dead. This trauma associated with drowning is one of my holes. I didn't know how much it impacted me until (many years later) my husband wanted to have "lake day." Dave grew up going to the lake, so he wanted to pass that love onto our children. We rented a boat and made big lake day plans. I had always hated lake day but didn't know why.

We were out floating on the water, with the kids swimming around underneath the boat's hull. Everyone was having a great time except me because I was a nervous wreck. Suddenly, I realized that I couldn't see my son.

"*Where's David? Does anyone see David?*" I started freaking out, my mind running toward the worst possible outcome. My body responded with adrenaline, mental fog, and a pit in my stomach. I frantically searched around the perimeter of the boat. And on the other side of the boat, I saw David pleasantly swimming along.

My husband asked, "What is going on?" I had to really sit back to think, *why did I respond like that? David's a good, strong swimmer. Why do I dread lake day?* Then it hit me. I was scared that my little boy had drowned because my cousin almost drowned so many years ago.

Dave and I needed to talk about how to best approach lake day now that I knew my hole (the fear of drowning due to the trauma of seeing my cousin almost die at the bottom of the pool). We recognized the hole for what it is: a past trauma that triggers present fear.

We resolved the conflict with a compromise. We would still do lake day as a family. I would stay on the boat for two hours and the kids would stay within my line of sight. Then, when the two hours passed, I would happily get dropped off at the dock and Dave would take the kids to do fun lake things that aren't so fun for me. Then I get to go home to relax for the rest of the day. It's a win-win.

I'd like to point out that I didn't always know the "why." For a long time, I hated lake day and would self-coach, telling myself "the lake's not scary--get over it!" Instead of trying to convince myself that I could get over it, I should have asked the question that leads to progress, "why?" When I finally asked this question, I put the pieces together, connecting my cousin almost drowning to my repulsion of lake day.

How can you know your hole? Whenever you feel overcome by anxiety, you may need to ask those, "why?" questions. You may know it now. To help you identify your hole(s), I'll list several that regularly come up in counseling: abuse, assault, trauma, addiction. On a less severe level, the hole could be thinking and wishing you were something else. For example, the hole could be introverts who think they're supposed to be extroverts, or short people who think they should be tall. Once you know your hole, you see the gap, the lack of ground on which you could build your home.

Unfortunately, we often try to fill our hole with sand instead of doing the difficult work of preparing and pouring a concrete foundation. We feel the pain of the hole and try to fill it with sand that occasionally goes by the name of sex, drugs, and/or alcohol. Other times it's with sand that goes by the name of control, anxiety, eating, or not eating.

Intuitively, you know you can't build a house over your hole, so you try to fill the hole with this sand. For a little while, the sand works. Your hole is full, and you don't feel those absences anymore. But when you try to build your house on that hole, the sand causes it to collapse. Sand doesn't give a foundation, but a short-term solution. It's like eating sugar when your body needs protein.

I wish I could give myself the credit for this "house on sand" analogy, but God said it first.

"And everyone who hears these words of mine and does not do them will be like a foolish man who built his house upon the sand; and the rain fell, and the floods came, and the winds blew and beat against that house, and it fell; and great was the fall of it." Gospel of St. Matthew, Chapter 7, verses 26-27.

A house built on sand lacks a sturdy foundation; it needs to be built on cement. Often, you try to fill your hole with sand repeatedly, more eagerly each time because your house fell again. The cycle perpetuates because you feel a pressing need to rebuild that causes you to fill the hole with whatever you can find... more sand. No matter how many times you try to fill your hole with sand, it will not be the solid foundation on which you need to build your house.

HOUSE ON SAND EXAMPLE

Imagine two people, newly engaged. His house is built on sand and so is hers. They have shared their sand with one another mutually accepting their future spouse's sand.

They feel like their love is enough for a foundation to keep their houses standing tall. They know marriage is hard, but they are great at keeping their hole full of sand. If they work hard enough to pack in the sand, everything will be okay.

Fast-forward six or twelve or twenty-four months - maybe more, maybe less. They are married. They now have two houses built on sand. The wife's house has sunk into the hole, so the husband's house is trying to hold up hers, but because his house lacks a sturdy foundation, the weight of both homes is too much for his sand to handle. Disaster! The homes fall in like a house of cards. They finally realize that no matter how hard they pack in the sand, their houses will keep falling without a solid foundation.

The lie anxiety tells us is that we can control everything so our house will never fall. Nothing bad will ever happen. But the reality is that we don't have control over everything. The only form of control we have is truly our self-control.

Often, people won't seek help from counseling until they are exhausted. They are exhausted from losing control, dumping sand into their hole over and over, and watching their house fall. They come to counseling with disheartened feelings, yet they carry an optimism that there must be something better.

The good news is that there is a better option! The counselor is there to help you build a strong foundation, one that can anchor your house. Would you try to build a house without working with a contractor, someone who is trained to build a house? You would want someone who has studied and practiced building foundations. A good contractor knows how to work with you, offer the right tools, and show you how to create the house of your dreams.

We need to fill these holes with something that will last. Let's stop the cycle, get rid of the sand, and build a basement. Knowing your hole and understanding the need for a reliable foundation is a huge accomplishment! Understanding why you respond to certain situations the way you do brings structure to your hole. You know what you're working with as opposed to blindly experiencing the effects of your hole. This knowledge and understanding of the hole as the root cause for your anxiety is akin to laying the foundation for your future basement.

Easier said than done, I know. The goal of Sacred Heart Mental Wellness is to help you gain understanding, and teach you tools and strategies to help you build a solid foundation for your house. I've built many mental wellness foundations in my time. So now it's time to walk with you. We will look at the biological activities in the brain to equip you to acknowledge whether or not you know the kind of sand in your life, or in the lives of those whom you love.

We'll come back to the holes and sand throughout this book. You'll learn strategies to remove the sand, build your basement, and have a strong foundation on which to build your home. I'm with you.

"There is in the
Sacred Heart
the symbol and express
image of the infinte
love of Jesus Christ
which moves us to love in
return."

- Pope Leo XIII

CHAPTER 2

THE ANXIOUS RESPONSE

CHAPTER 2 | THE ANXIOUS RESPONSE

BRAIN BIOLOGY

Learning about the biological activity (on a very basic level because the brain is a beautifully complex organ) will help you see anxiety as one kind of sand that can fill your hole. This is the first step in the right direction to work through the sand and get to the point where you can build a strong foundation for your house.

Often people ask the question, if God made me to be enough, and my mind is good, then why can't I just stop feeling anxious? To understand anxiety, you must know a little about the brain and its biological responses. Let me explain.

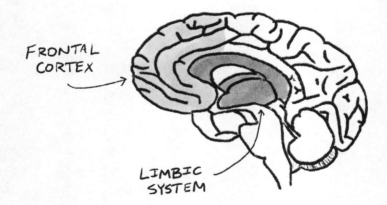

The frontal cortex is in the front of the brain. This is the part of your brain responsible for decision-making, high-level thinking, as well as your personality. I will also refer to the frontal cortex as the "thinking brain" because of its ability to process information and make decisions with that information.

The limbic system is in the center of your brain. God cleverly designed it to be the most safeguarded part of your brain. The limbic system must be protected because its job is to keep you alive. It regulates your heart rate, blood pressure, keeps you breathing, and all the things you are too busy to think about! I'll refer to this system as the "animal brain" because it primarily reacts to stimuli; it does not "think."

ANXIOUS RESPONSES ARE GOOD

God created the frontal cortex and the limbic system to work together. When they cooperate, it's called the anxious response. This is when your animal brain senses a dangerous stimuli, which triggers the release of stress hormones throughout your body. These hormones cause you to fly, fight, and/or freeze. I'm going to show how this process works in a real-life scenario.

BEAR EXAMPLE

Imagine you are hiking in the woods. You spot a huge grizzly bear. You can see his teeth, smell the fur, and hear his steps breaking the branches that cover the forest floor. These senses go up to your animal brain and say, *Bear! Bear! Bear! He sees me! He's going to eat me! I'm going to die!*

Your body immediately responds. You rack your brain to remember what to do when you see a grizzly bear. *Do I run? Do I play dead? Do I try to climb a tree?* Your heart is pounding, and you feel more energized than ever before; your heart is creating more oxygenated blood so you can run fast, jump high, or do whatever it takes to survive this bear. Your digestive system comes to a screeching halt, but you don't notice this until later. You feel like you're trapped inside your body, like you're about to explode with pent up energy. This is the rush of adrenaline you'll need to stand a chance against this bear. But your mind is hazy because you don't know what to do. And that mental fog is a good thing for your survival because if you calculated the odds of you fighting and winning against a grizzly bear... it wouldn't look so good.

All these responses come from the stress hormones sourced in the animal brain. God created your mind this way to help you survive in life-or-death situations. You were created so intentionally because God desires your good. He wants you to survive. Furthermore, He wants you to know and appreciate the animal brain's response to danger. Let's take another look at these biological responses.

FIGHT, FLIGHT, OR FREEZE
BIOLOGICAL STRESS RESPONSES

STRESS RESPONSE:	WHY IS THIS HAPPENING?
Heart rate increases	Your body needs as much oxygen as possible if you're going to run from a bear.
Digestion slows down	Your body will conserve energy so you have the stamina to fight the bear. (This often leads to stomach troubles.)
'Tiger in a cage' feeling	Adrenaline is pumping through your muscles to get you ready. You will be wide awake and alert so you can fight the bear.
Mental fog	Your thinking brain and animal brain are not clearly communicating. This is a good thing because if they were on the same page and you thought about the probability of outrunning the bear, you're probably not going to run or fight... and that's not going to end well.

If you have ever felt anxious, you may relate to feelings of the stress response.

WHY YOU CAN'T THINK YOUR WAY OUT

Sometimes, your thinking brain and animal brain are on separate pages. Your body responds to a perceived dangerous stimulus; the animal brain commits to fight, flight, or freeze. It sends stress hormones throughout your body. Meanwhile, your frontal cortex is thinking, *I know I am safe, so I'll just try to think myself out of the anxiety.* You can try to think your way out, but it doesn't work that way. Your animal brain senses a danger, while the thinking brain knows you're safe. This discrepancy causes your thinking and animal brains to get into a fight about whether or not you are safe. This conflict is where anxiety lies.

Here's why you can't think yourself out of the anxiety. Remember the mental fog response? God drew the curtain between your thinking brain and animal brain so you could survive. As a result, you do not have control over your animal brain, or the stress hormones being pumped into your body. Your thinking brain does not have the power to tell your animal brain to stop even though you may be safe.

A little unsure about the whole 'thinking brain doesn't control the animal brain' issue? Let's experiment.

THINKING vs. ANIMAL BRAIN EXPERIMENT

<u>Directions</u>:

Close your eyes and try with all your thinking brain power to stop your heartbeat. Observe the results.

Seriously, try this right now.

Did you do it?

You may be giggling right now because you can't stop your heart by sheer will power. Your thinking brain does not have control over your animal brain, and this is a very good thing! Do me a favor and hold onto that giggle. Perspective and a sense of humor are important for handling your anxious response.

NERVOUS SYSTEM

We are taught from a young age about the senses: eyes see, noses smell, mouths taste, ears hear, and hands feel. Additionally, the nerves in your sensory organs sense stimuli. They send the sensed stimulus up the spinal cord, which runs right into the animal brain. There, the animal brain acts like a post office. It looks at the address, where the stimulus is to be received and sends it there. However, when danger is perceived, the animal brain doesn't have time to send the message to the thinking brain to get approval. In God's great plan to keep you safe and alive, the animal brain reacts first by pumping stress hormones throughout your body. Secondarily, the animal brain lets your thinking brain know what all the commotion is about.

PASTA ANALOGY

You're cooking pasta. It's in a boiling pot on the stove. You can see steam swirling off the top, and smell the starchy aroma. You need to feel and taste the pasta to see if it's perfectly *al dente*. You reach for a noodle but it's too hot to handle! This sensation goes to your animal brain, and you drop the pasta and move your hand back.

At the same time, your animal brain sends the message to your thinking brain, "It's too hot!"

In this analogy, you don't need to think *"it's too hot"* for you to move your hand. Your body simply reacted in defense. This reactionary response is the animal brain at work. This is just the way God intended it to happen, to help you even before you know you need help. This response is often one (or more) of the three: fight, flight, or freeze. In the pasta analogy, we saw the flight response. You immediately responded to get your hand away from the source of danger.

God made your body this way so you could act (in a life-saving way) before thinking yourself out of it. The feelings you have when you feel anxious are the same as the ones when you have flight, fight, or freeze. We assume that these feelings are always bad, but in many situations, they are good and protect us. God made it this way so we could live and live fully!

PASTA ANALOGY – FLIPPED

If the thinking brain dictated instructions to the animal brain, the pasta analogy would play out differently. You would reach for the pasta. Your fingers are in the boiling water, and you would need to think, *it's too hot*. I should do something about that. What should I do? Maybe I'll take my hand out. That will make me feel better.

Meanwhile, your hand is burning in the boiling water! You tried to think yourself out of the situation. But in the time it took to run the thoughts through your mind, your hand has already been burnt and severely injured!

Your animal brain is good, and necessary for your well-being. It is good and beautiful that your thinking brain cannot control it.

DEFINITION OF ANXIETY

Let's get down to it. We've seen examples where the animal brain acts for the good, releasing the anxious response stress hormones so it can help us survive. The animal brain is always acting on good intentions, but sometimes it releases stress hormones when we're not in dangerous situations. In other words, your animal brain senses danger and sends your body into survival mode, while your thinking brain recognizes that you're safe. <u>Anxiety is the experience of fear, worry, or unease that results from the release of the animal brain's stress hormones even though the thinking brain acknowledges your safety.</u> Note here that anxiety is also a form of sand often used to fill a hole.

PUBLIC SPEAKING EXAMPLE

You may need to give a public speech at work. Right before you go front and center you get hit with the animal brain's stress hormones. Your palms may get sweaty. You may feel frozen in time. You may sense a rush of adrenaline. You may even feel the desire to hide.

You know you are safe, but you are anxious because your animal brain senses danger. In this example, you fear the consequence of potentially making a mistake, being publicly corrected, and not being perfect in every way. The thought would be... if I mess up on this talk, I could lose my job and then become homeless, then starve to death and die. This "stuck on a hamster wheel" way of thinking happens instantly, and most people do not even know their animal brain has gone this far down the rabbit hole.

Hold on. This is where I need you to remember the giggle, how you felt when you realized you couldn't control your animal brain. You're not alone in this.

We see these (perceived) flaws, and fall into the cycle of thinking, *I will never be enough*. The thought rolls over and over in your head and heart as you intake social media, advertisements, and most marketing strategies. Let me draw it out for you.

FASHION TREND EXAMPLE

During the fall season that this book is being written, the fashion trend is wide leg pants. Skinny jeans are out. Wide leg is in. Now, one could feed into this trend because they genuinely like wide leg pants. No big deal. But if you are buying a shopping cart full of wide leg pants while mourning the loss of your skinny jeans, you are probably falling for the lie that says, I will never be enough. In your mind, you may not outright think *"I'm not enough"*, but it will come in the form of *"I want to look like the influencers on Instagram"*, or *"I want to look like that (whatever your ideal might be)"* or *"once I have these jeans I'll finally keep up with the times. Then I'll be happy."*

Marketing is all about telling you what you have, and who you are is not enough. We happen to live in a world that operates on you believing you're not enough. The economy would collapse if everyone stopped following fashion trends, perfectly decorating the house to match the trends, getting the master's degree purely for the prestige, or buying that new car just because you're tired of your old one. The goal of marketing is to create the feeling of lack, so we can spend money to fill that hole. In reality, excess spending or "shopping therapy" is a type of sand.

We live in a society that constantly needs external affirmation to feel like we are enough, accepted, and loved. Imagine if we didn't. What if we lived in a world where people started believing they were enough and stopped buying those new jeans to make them worthy of love. To recall, Satan is a liar who tries to drive this fear of not being enough into society (especially the women).

So, what can we do?

Start by recognizing that the lies are sourced in the father of all lies. Call Satan's bluff. See the lies, cast them out, and reclaim the truth! God designed the mind to be good and He did it because He loves us. Clinging onto the truth that God made you good and whole is the perfect place to start! Knowing you are created good and that you are loved is your home base for overcoming anxiety and cultivating a life of mental wellness.

SUMMARY

Anxiety occurs when the limbic system (animal brain) gets scared and thinks you're going to die even though you are safe. The animal brain goes into survival mode by pumping stress hormones into your body. You feel the adrenaline, stomach troubles, tiger in a cage feeling, and the mental fog preparing you to fight, fly, or freeze.

In life-or-death situations, your animal brain can save you. However, your life is probably safe most of the time. So, when the anxiety hits and the animal brain is releasing stress hormones, your frontal cortex (thinking brain) says, *"it's just a (insert a situation that gives you anxiety). I am safe. Why am I freaking out? Am I crazy?"*

No. You're not crazy. We've discussed the lack of communication carried out by your frontal cortex and limbic system. You can recognize this miscommunication and you are able to see where your anxiety stems. Your body is responding when it perceives a sense of danger. God created your animal brain to propel you toward survival at all costs. He loves you and wants you to live! He is good and you are created good.

Nevertheless, you might be feeling discouraged. Stay with me and don't lose hope! Instead of working against these truths, work with them. It's important for you to acknowledge the sand in your life. Know that everyone has a hole, the negative past experiences or thoughts that make you feel like you're not enough. This gap is felt, so you try to fill it with the sand of control, or anxiety, maybe you fill it with shopping, or eating.

Reflect on your life to identify the sand you are using to fill those holes. Recognizing and removing your sand will help lessen your feelings of anxiety.

Calling back to the house on sand analogy, the next section will offer strategies that will be your tools to work through the sand. Some tools will help you remove the sand and start building a new foundation for your mental wellness. This foundation will help you process the stimuli your body is experiencing in a new way, while the tools help you frame out the basement with 2x4's. Soon you will have a solid foundation with a framed-out basement!

With Christ as your guide in this process, know that your basement will be filled with truth and goodness. He will be your cornerstone on which you build your life. The strategies you're about to read, practice, and practice again are based in science, Biblical wisdom, and clinical experience. They will change your life and the way you manage anxiety!

"Cling to God,
and leave all the rest to
Him. He will not let you
perish. Your soul is very
dear to Him.
He wishes to save it."

- St. Margaret Mary Alacoque

CHAPTER 3

STRATEGIES

CHAPTER 3 | STRATEGIES

HAMSTER WHEEL

If you've skipped ahead to this section without starting from the beginning of this book, please stop. Go back to the beginning. Trust the process. The strategies will not help you if you don't have the context for why they work.

For those who have trusted the process, you'll know that the fight, flight, or freeze response, in and of itself, is good. Remember, it can save you from an encounter with a bear. But in your generally safe daily life, it becomes anxiety, a thorn in your side instead of the flight, fight, or freeze response meant to save you. Therefore, you need to learn how to avoid feeding into the anxiety.

Recall the anxiety-filled scenario: The burn on your finger from the boiling pasta water is real. The pain is real; but your life is not in danger. Anxiety leads you to have a train of thoughts that quickly escalate.

EXAMPLE: VOICE OF THE HAMSTER WHEEL

"I didn't study enough for this test. Oh no! I don't know the answer to #1!"

"I'm scared! I'm going to die!"

"I feel anxious. Oh no! Now I'm anxious because I'm anxious! And that makes me feel even more anxious that I'm anxious because I'm anxious!"

"I'm going to fail this test. Then I'm going to fail this class. Then I'm going to fail this semester. I'm going to become a college dropout. Then I'll be homeless, and no one will love me!"

"I'll never be enough!"

Anxiety can be the cycle of living in the past or fearing the present. Feeding into the anxiety will cause a faster and stronger hormone response, which is like an out-of-control hamster on a wheel. For this hamster (or for you) it may feel as though there is no end in sight. The more the hamster runs, the more it must keep running. But the truth is, you don't have to keep running!

Getting off the wheel (stopping the cycle of these detrimental thoughts) is good and must be done intentionally. I want to help you stop running by utilizing strategies that will help stop the continuous hormone release. Recognizing these thoughts as a never-ending cycle is a huge first step. You can't manipulate your animal brain's lack of communication to your thinking brain, so you must work with what you can control: your thinking brain.

By utilizing your thinking brain's knowledge of the biology of anxiety, you can be empowered to get off the hamster wheel. You will be able to tell yourself, *I'm not crazy. It's not my fault. It's out of my control. I am enough.* From there, you can free yourself from the hamster wheel of anxiety.

The sooner you stop the line of thinking caused by anxiety, the sooner you will start to feel the stress responses decrease. Once you're out of the anxious cycle of thinking, you can take proactive steps to regain your sense of calm. Cultivating this recognition and skill helps to remove some of the sand. On the wheel, the anxious cycle of thinking causes a sandstorm that blocks your ability to see a way out. But when you consciously stop thinking, you clear a path. You remove some of the lies and allow yourself to get off the wheel.

STRATEGIES

In the following section, I offer strategies. Some will help slow down the production of the stress hormones so that you can start to regain your sense of calm and peace. Some will be helpful once you're already off the hamster wheel. For example, you're probably not going to take deep breaths if your mind is racing, saying, *I'm going to die!* They all have a time and place, at different times and places.

These strategies are not new information, or magic ideas. That said, they are as effective as you are intentional with their implementation. To aid in your intentionality with these strategies, I'll explain the why and the how they communicate safety to your brain.

Secondly, do not try to use all twelve strategies for a single bout of anxiety. Use what works for you. Each strategy might be helpful in your life, but they will most likely be helpful at different times and places. I am providing options so you can best utilize the strategy for your current stage in life.

Lastly, you must give yourself time. You're not going to feel better instantaneously. Stress hormones must be processed through the body. It may take up to twenty minutes for the hormones to metabolize into your body - and that's okay. They need to go through your system almost like alcohol must be processed for you to regain sobriety. The first chunk of time when hormones are being released will probably be spent on the hamster wheel. The better you get at recognizing "*I am safe*" the sooner you can start managing the feelings of anxiety. Your brain is beautifully created; therefore, it is complicated!

STRATEGIES

1. Thank God for your anxiety

2. Claim Safety

3. Recognition

4. Do Not Fear

5. Deep Breathing

6. Grounding

7. Neuroplasticity

8. Journaling

9. Exercise

10. Healthy Eating

11. Imagery

12. The Cross

13. Adoration

14. Rosary

15. Your Net

STRATEGY #1 | THANK GOD FOR YOUR ANXIETY

RECOMMENDED USE: before, during, and after experiencing anxiety.

I know this one brings up a lot of feelings since so many hate their anxiety. But it is such an important step for overcoming your hole, getting off the hamster wheel, and building your house!

Say this prayer or something similar. (Several prayers to the Sacred Heart of Jesus are printed in the appendix at the end of the book.)

> *Thank You, Jesus, for my anxiety. I know that You made me good and that You love me. I trust in You. Amen.*

Praying with the intentionality that I know this part of my brain is good, I am created good, and I can be thankful to God for wanting to keep me safe, helps me to remember that. The intentionality behind the words reminds you that this is not your fault, you are not bad, crazy, or weak. Your animal brain got scared and you must reassure it of safety.

PRACTICE

Throughout the day, offer short spontaneous prayers. You could make it up as you go, depending on the situation. If you like a little more structure, set a reminder on your phone to go off at 7am, 12pm, 3pm, and 6pm. The reminders could have the prayer visible on the notification. The reminders could read:

Thank you for today, Jesus.

Jesus, I love you. Thank you for loving me.

Jesus, I trust in you.

Jesus, I need you.

I trust that I am beautifully and wonderfully made.

The point - practice calling out to Jesus so your life is unrecognizable apart from him. He loves you and wants to carry your cross with you.

STRATEGY #2 | CLAIM SAFETY

RECOMMENDED USE: before, during, and after experiencing anxiety.

This strategy is one to use once you identify the experience of anxiety. Use your thinking brain to internally repeat, animal brain, *I am safe.*

This is a concrete way to help your mind get off the hamster wheel. You will want to address your animal in self-talk as a cue for the brain, letting it know you are safe. Be aware that you will have to override your thinking brain with sheer willpower because it will communicate, *of course I am safe. Why am I talking to myself?* It's okay to giggle a little when this happens. You are sane and healthy - you might need to convince yourself of it!

These words will slowly translate to your animal brain, and the anxiety will subside. You must give it time. The stress hormones released at the onset of anxiety will have to course through your body. The sooner you can convince your animal brain of your safety, the sooner the response will end.

PRACTICE

Slowly and calmly repeat the phrase: *I am safe.* Continue until you say it slowly and calmly, as many times as you need. It may help to say it silently or out loud, which makes this strategy a good one to use while in public.

I am safe. I am safe. I am safe.

STRATEGY #3 | RECOGNITION

RECOMMENDED USE: during the experience of anxiety.

Sometimes, your brain senses stimuli that you are unaware of. It may sound like this; *I don't know why I feel anxious. I think I'm going crazy!*

When this happens, know that a stimuli is going to your animal brain but your thinking brain says, *eh, it's not important. We're not even going to acknowledge it.* Therefore, one has anxiety because their animal brain releases stress hormones without the message being acknowledged by the thinking brain. Therefore, you can be anxious without knowing the reason why.

EXAMPLE

If I tell you, *you are wearing clothes.* Suddenly, you realize the weight of your clothing; the texture is felt on your skin. You recognize that you are, in fact, wearing clothes. But before I told you, you weren't consciously aware of your clothing.

Your thinking brain doesn't waste the mental energy repeating the fact, *I have clothes on, I have clothes on, I have clothes on*, all day long. Thank goodness! You don't have the mental space to be taken up by obvious statements. You have so many more good things to fill your mind with than, *I have clothes on.*

Remember that you are a human and you are created good. In this scenario, your body is responding to an animal brain distress signal, but your thinking brain never got the message. Simply recognizing this biological fact as a phenomenon is a tool to help you get off the hamster wheel.

PERSONAL EXAMPLE

Sometimes when I try to go to sleep, I have anxiety. My husband will say, "Catherine, you're the anxiety counseling queen. You've spoken on the topic and helped so many people. Why do you have anxiety?"

I proceed to tell him, "Last time I checked, I still have an animal brain that I have no control over that might have sensed something dangerous." I recognize it and step off the hamster wheel before the anxiety gets carried away.

PRACTICE

The ability to implement recognition needs to be ready to go at a moment's notice. So, practice by remembering throughout the day, *I have an animal brain. I have no control over the response and hormone release, but I do have control over how I react to them and the next steps I take. My brain is trying to keep me safe. I am healthy. I am good.*

When the anxiety is triggered, your mind should be prepared to make sense of the stress hormones being released into your body. You remember you have no control. Therefore, recognition is a solid first step before utilizing another strategy like deep breathing or grounding so you can speak to your animal brain through the senses it receives.

STRATEGY #4 | DO NOT FEAR

RECOMMENDED USE: before, during, and after experiencing anxiety.

Fearing anxiety will instigate more fear. Then you become fearful of having anxiety because it gives you anxiety. All you're left with in this situation is more anxiety. You can't let yourself get stuck on the hamster wheel because of this.

Your anxiety came from a dangerous stimulus to the animal brain. You will know you're off the hamster wheel when you let that sense of danger be the focus, not your battle against anxiety. It's time to move from fear into confidence and acceptance.

MILITARY ANALOGY

You're in the military. Your time is broken down to 98% training, 1% paperwork, and 1% fighting. When joining the military, you probably don't want to go to war. You may fear going to war, but you accept the fact you might have to go fight for your country. Because the possibility of war is acknowledged, the military dedicates more time for training than anything else. They want their men and women equipped so they can be confident and successful instead of letting fear impose on their mission.

Anxiety is similar in that no one wants to be anxious. You may fear anxiety, which is only going to make you more anxious. But if you accept the fact that anxiety will happen, you can train yourself to be calm and prepared for when it decides to rear its ugly face. You'll have the grace and courage to face your hole instead of packing it full of sand.

PRACTICE

Approach anxiety as an attempted natural process meant to be good and lifesaving. The more this idea is embraced, the more natural it will be to deal with it when in crisis. One of your goals could be getting to the point where you say, "I'm going to have anxiety and that's okay because I have tools to manage it, and the skills to overcome it. I don't have to fight it alone. I am intentionally created this way for a purpose!" with the spirit of acceptance and confidence.

STRATEGY #5 | DEEP BREATHING

RECOMMENDED USE: before, during, and after experiencing anxiety.

As a counselor, I hear people laugh at, or blow off deep breathing like it doesn't work. If you don't know why you are doing something (like taking deep breaths) it's not going to work. However, if you understand why you are doing something it is usually more productive.

So, here's the 'why.' When you take deep breaths, it slows your heart rate. The key is to talk to your animal brain in the language it speaks, which is through the senses. You must show your animal brain that it's safe for your heart rate to steady, there is no imminent danger. This strategy will help you get off the hamster wheel. The more you practice it (before and after you experience anxiety) the more naturally you'll step off that hamster wheel.

PRACTICE

Close your eyes and take three slow breaths to start. In and out, in and out, in and out. As you breathe, focus on your heart rate. Use your thinking brain to focus on slowing your breath so your animal brain gets the message that you are safe.

Repeat as often as necessary. This is an exercise you can do in the privacy of your home, or in a sea of people. You can practice deep breathing in a final interview, sitting across from your in-laws, before going to sleep at night, literally anywhere at any time! It's one of my favorites because this strategy is something you can do to manage your anxiety no matter where you are located.

STRATEGY #6 | GROUNDING

RECOMMENDED USE: before, especially during, and after experiencing anxiety.

Many times, when you're during anxiety, the worst-case scenarios flood your mind. Our feelings of anxiety can cause irrational fears and playing these fears out in your head will lead to more anxiety. If the goal is to get off the hamster wheel, a tool to practice is simply being present. Grounding is a quick way to bring your senses to the present moment, recognizing where you are so your animal brain knows you're safe. Your thinking brain can speak the language of the animal brain by focusing on what you can touch, taste, see, feel, and hear.

If you really need a dose of reality, bite into a lemon. The sour taste shocks your system and draws you out of that irrational head space. Instead, you become present to the sour lemony taste.

You don't need a lemon to use this strategy. Grounding simply requires that you take notice of where you are. If you have anxiety in a public setting, grounding (and deep breathing) is a silent exercise you may do without needing to step out of the room or drawing attention. The more you practice grounding, the quicker and easier it will come.

PRACTICE

Observe your surroundings through your senses. To do so, identify one stimulus per sense. You can be as broad or detailed as what's helpful to you.

Go ahead. I'll give you my responses for an example.

What do you feel?	My old flannel shirt
What do you hear?	My son playing with his rattle
What do you see?	A cup of iced water
What do you smell?	Rain
What do you taste?	Aftertaste of a freshly baked chocolate chip cookie

STRATEGY #7 | NEUROPLASTICITY

RECOMMENDED USE: before, during, and after experiencing anxiety.

The ideas of neuroplasticity mean your brain is dynamic. It is not stuck, unable to learn, grow, nor develop. Your brain is constantly changing, creating connections, new neuropathways, or losing the ones previously established.

EXAMPLE

Think of a stroke patient. They had a stroke which caused them to lose the connections in the brain that enable them to speak. However, the brain can adapt and start creating different, new connections to relearn how to communicate.

Another way this concept may be referenced is neuropathways. These connections will do whatever you or your experience has trained them to do. If your brain has been trained to believe test taking is scary, your mind will continue to think within that pattern until you intentionally chisel out a new neuropathway. If you can rewire your thinking from, I'm not good enough, to *I am strong, resilient, and safe*, you will change the way your brain responds to the animal brain's stress hormones. You will be able to recognize the onset of anxiety more quickly each time and be equipped to implement whichever strategy works for you. The faster your thinking brain recognizes anxiety, the faster you will be able to get off the hamster wheel.

EXAMPLE

The first time you drive, every step, every adjustment is calculated. You make sure everything is just right for you to successfully drive a lap around the school parking lot on Saturday morning. It is all very intentional. I remember the first time I drove. I went three miles and required a nap afterwards because I was concentrating so hard. Fast forward to the present. Now I can drive all over Timbuktu and not even think about how to drive the car.

As you learn something new, offer repetition. In doing so you can strengthen your neuropathways.

PRACTICE

You can practice this concept by repeating the truth to yourself.

If you're nervous about driving, you can say your script, *I am wearing my seatbelt. I am in control. I am safe.*

If you're about to take a test you can say, *I studied. I know the material. I am going to do the best I can.*

If you don't want to move across the country for your spouse, say, *"Jesus, I trust in you. I know that You are good, and You want good for me."*

STRATEGY #8 | JOURNALING

RECOMMENDED USE: before, sometimes during, and after experiencing anxiety.

Writing is a proactive way to get your thoughts out of your head and on paper (or a typed document). When a concept is in your head it can be whatever you want.

EXAMPLE

Growing up, I watched a lot of college volleyball on TV. I wanted to be the tall blonde that could hit and set. In my mind, I would be the one who could be the double threat for the team. I could decide in a split second to feed the ball to the hitter or surprise my opponent by smacking it over on the second hit, straight to the floor. In my mind, I was the six-foot, blonde, left-handed setter on the volleyball court. I can think these things with all my might! But my short, Puerto Rican, and right-handed self cannot be those things in reality!

What I saw on TV created this ideal image of my dream self. My aspirations turned into a, *this is how I should be*, way of thinking instead of being grateful for how God made me. The lie circulated, leading me to the belief that I was bad, and no good.

In reality, I was a dang good back row player that played at nationals in club volleyball. I wish I could go back to my young, teenage self to say: The ideas you have about who you should be shouldn't come from the media, you should look to the Creator to see how intentionally and lovely He made you. You don't need to be tall, blonde, and flawless to be enough. I offer the grace that makes you more than enough.

Journaling is good at helping you exterminate the unwanted thoughts and fears from your mind and heart. Trapped in your head the lies can seem true, so you stay on the hamster wheel. But when you write them down, and cross them off, or rip them up, and see the frailty of the lies, the truth shines through. This truth breaks the spinning cycle of the hamster wheel so you can walk freely in the truth.

GARDENING ANALOGY

Sometimes I like to think of our minds like a garden. I don't know if you've ever gardened, but here in Kansas everyone gardens.

I decided, I'm here, I want to garden. So, I got this 20 x 20 garden. In the Springtime I got all these beautiful plants and in the Spring it's so pretty! You can tell there's no wind, no heat, and there are no bugs. But by July, it gets hot. And the weeds grow so fast! No matter how often I try to pluck them, they keep growing and I can't keep up. So, then I decided I'm going to stop weeding. By August, I don't know what's a vegetable or what's a weed. I can't even see my plants anymore.

Our mind is kind of like this. When we keep all our thoughts inside it's hard to decipher between the weeds that we must pull out and the vegetables that we must work with.

By journaling you can take those abstract thoughts and write them out. Then, even if you decide to throw the paper away, you can pinpoint the truth. Recognizing these truths expose the lies which send a domino effect toward the irrational fears harbored in your heart. Then these fears are exposed, called out, and replaced by truth.

PRACTICE

Pull out a piece of paper, or a blank document on your computer/phone/tablet. Jot down a list of what's on your mind. You could describe joys, fears, insecurities, ideas, etc. Be brutally honest with yourself. No one needs to see this list.

Now, sift through your thoughts. Which are lies? Which are truths? Claim the lies, give them to Jesus, and ask St. Michael the Archangel to fight this battle for you. Pope Leo XIII (1884) wrote this prayer you can cling to:

Saint Michael the Archangel, defend us in battle. Be our protection against the wickedness and snares of the devil; May God rebuke him, we humbly pray; And do thou, O Prince of the Heavenly Host, by the power of God, thrust into hell Satan and all evil spirits who prowl about the world seeking the ruin of souls. Amen.

Thank God for the truths you wrote down and hold tight onto them. Don't just go through the motions but use them to allow God to carry this cross with you. I recommend placing this list next to a statue of Jesus or Mary. They will take care of the highs and lows on your heart, taking care of you for the night while you rest.

STRATEGY #9 | EXERCISE

RECOMMENDED USE: before, during, and after experiencing anxiety.

I know it's not everyone's favorite. I wish I liked exercise more than I do.

But when those stress hormones are in your system, you are ready to fight bears. Remember your body's response is fight, flight, or freeze. Your hormones are preparing you to run as fast as you can or fight with every calorie of energy your body contains. Instead of letting this energy drive you crazy on the hamster wheel, get it out. Your body is prepared for physical exertion, so let it happen. Do some push-ups, sit ups, or even a short walk. Do what you need to do to flex those muscles. Then your body can use those stress hormones for what they are meant to do!

Exercise also increases the endorphins in your body. These "feel-good" hormones are what you experience after a good work out. They help reduce stress and give you a little pep in your step, which are great for getting off the hamster wheel. Also, when you exercise your mind is focused on the task at hand. Whether it is your squatting form, engaging your core during a plank, or running to the end of the next block, your focus is on something other than what causes the anxiety. While your thinking brain is occupied in your workout, your animal brain receives new senses that communicate safety.

PRACTICE

Do the following: 10 push-ups   10 squats

10 sit-ups   30 second wall sit

Notice that you are now focused on the short workout. When you are in an anxiety-filled situation, your body's stress hormones will have been put to good use.

STRATEGY #10 | HEALTHY EATING

RECOMMENDED USE: before, and after experiencing anxiety.

Before explaining this strategy, please do not become anxious about your diet. Take a deep breath. All I want to talk about is awareness of caffeine and sugar. Eating causes a rise in blood sugar. This is natural and good for your body to healthily function. What one eats deeply impacts the bodily response.

EXAMPLE

At the VET Center when I worked with Veterans with PTSD, I'd hear a client say, "I'm anxious and jittery. I can't sleep at night!" I would proceed to ask them about their eating and sleeping habits. "Well...I have about seven mountain dews a day. I eat a donut before bed. I drink espresso..." I see the issue here, and I'm guessing you can see it too. They were already on high alert due to past experiences, but the sugars paired with the caffeine intake were not helping at all.

Awareness of what you consume and how it affects your body is a low-level strategy that can be extremely beneficial to you. Here's how it works.

Additional sugar and caffeine cause your blood sugar to go through a roller coaster, causing your energy to ride the peaks and valleys of said roller coaster. When your blood sugar crashes because the caffeine or sugar is depleted, your mood and energy plummet. This can open the door for anxiety to spike and the hamster wheel to spin.

Another notable factor is the hormone serotonin. This is another "feel-good" hormone that jumps with sugar intake and is inhibited with caffeine. Therefore, having an abundance of caffeine decreases your serotonin level, which can make you more prone to feeling anxious. With this knowledge, don't increase your sugar intake. The sugar high will need to come down at some point and it will end up at lower levels than where it started.

I would like to restate here that this is not a reason to be anxious. You do not need to cut all sugar and caffeine out of your life. If you feel you are consuming too much, gradually change your 8 daily cups of coffee to 2, and the big bowl of ice cream to a single scoop. Your body will thank you.

PRACTICE

Little steps can empower you. Try to make little decisions to fuel your body throughout the day. Knowing the effects of sugar and caffeine can help guide you when making decisions to help decrease the effects of anxiety.

STRATEGY #11 | IMAGERY

RECOMMENDED USE: before, especially during, and after experiencing anxiety.

Something most don't realize is the strength of your imagination. It is one of your strongest memory tools. For this strategy, take a memory you have of a time you felt safe, and run it through each of your senses. The trick with imagery is to take your memory and use your imagination to go through all the associated senses. Activating your senses will convince your animal brain that you are safe and it's safe to step off the hamster wheel.

PERSONAL EXAMPLE 1

It's best to have a go-to memory you can pull up at a moment's notice. One memory I use when I feel anxious is from our house in Pennsylvania. It had an old swing on the porch that I loved.

I can feel the roughness of the chair on the swing and taste the bitterness of my coffee. I can smell the pollen, it's thick enough you could wipe it up. (If you're from the East Coast you'll know what I mean!) I can hear the squeaking of the old chains as we rock back and forth. I can see the grass blowing in the wind. All is well.

PERSONAL EXAMPLE 2

I like to think about the old church that I visited in Ireland. I see the monstrance glowing with soft light, the sound of the silence, the feelings of the old hard pews, the taste of the cold damp air in the old stone church, and the smell of the candles burning.

PRACTICE

If you have a memory that includes apple pie, bring it to mind now.

Can you see a hot apple pie out of the oven? Can you smell the sweetness of the gooey apple filling? Can you hear the oven door closing as your Gram sets the pie safely on the table? Can you taste the cinnamon and apple paired with a crumb topping? Can you feel the warm, sweet apple on your tongue? (I intentionally picked a pie with the crumb topping because that's the only kind of apple pie I have in my world!)

Now, it's time to choose your go-to memory. This doesn't need to be the only memory you ever use for the rest of your life! I want you to temporarily pick a memory where you felt most like yourself, a time where you felt the most peace. Here are a few more examples to get the ball rolling.

Farmers might think about moving cattle. They might imagine the smell of money (that's how farmers reconcile with the smell of manure), they would picture the herd walking along the road, they could feel the grit on their teeth from the dust being kicked up. They may taste the fresh, open air as they hear moo's coming from the cattle.

Runners may feel the breeze and taste the sweat dripping into their mouth. They smell the pine trees on either side as their feet pound the trail, watching the forest disappear behind them.

Hopefully, you have a favorite memory chosen. I would encourage you to practice this strategy now, before you need it. Practice imagery when you are not experiencing anxiety, which will allow it to come easier when your animal brain is in fight, flight, or freeze response mode.

STRATEGY #12 | THE CROSS

RECOMMENDED USE: before, during, and after experiencing anxiety.

I love being Catholic. It's just the best! One of my favorite things about it is that the more I learn about mental health, the more I know God made the Church for us. He knows human struggle and gives you the tools to overcome anxiety! He loves you so much that He has equipped you to be the healthiest and happiest version of yourself.

It is important to talk about ways to bring anxiety to the cross. Before I can do that, look at what Scripture says about anxiety.

Therefore I tell you, do not be anxious about your life, what you shall eat or what you shall drink, nor about your body, what you shall put on. Is not life more than food, and the body more than clothing? Look at the birds of the air: they neither sow nor reap nor gather into barns, and yet your heavenly Father feeds them. Are you not of more value than they? And which of you by being anxious can add one cubit to his span of life? And why are you anxious about clothing? Consider the lilies of the field, how they grow; they neither toil nor spin; yet I tell you, even Solomon in all his glory was not arrayed like one of these. But if God so clothes the grass of the field, which today is alive and tomorrow is thrown into the oven, will he not much more clothe you, O men of little faith? Therefore do not be anxious, saying, 'What shall we eat?' or 'What shall we drink?' or 'What shall we wear?' For the Gentiles seek all these things; and your heavenly Father knows that you need them all. But seek first his kingdom and his righteousness, and all these things shall be yours as well. Therefore do not be anxious about tomorrow, for tomorrow will be anxious for itself. Let the day's own trouble be sufficient for the day. Gospel of St. Matthew Chapter 6, verses 25-34

God never said you wouldn't worry. He does say, when you worry, come to the cross. Come to me and let me take care of that for you. I'm here and I'm going to be with you.

One of the ways the Church can walk with you is through spiritual direction. This consists of regular meetings held between you and a qualified person. The qualified person could be a priest, religious brother or sister, or a trained lay person. Their role is to walk with you on your spiritual journey. At your meeting, you could discuss spiritual consolation, desolation, discernment, prayer, or other happenings in your spiritual life. This person is usually not trained as a counselor or psychologist, so only seek their expertise in the spiritual life.

That said, human nature is a union of body and spirit, created in the image and likeness of God. If your spirit is oriented toward Jesus, your mind and body will be sure to follow.

For example, when you reconcile yourself with God in the sacrament of Reconciliation, you come face to face (or behind the screen) with the priest who is acting *in persona Christi*, which means, in the person of Christ. Through the sacraments, God is granting you grace to experience Him. He offers himself to you, Love itself, in each prayer, sacrament, and sacrifice. This grace will reinforce the way you see yourself as someone who, by the grace of God, is good. Furthermore, the conviction of this goodness will help you get off the hamster wheel.

I am going to speak frankly and sound like a mom for a second. That priest is going to be so excited to see you. He doesn't care who you are or what you've done. He's heard it all (and more) before! All he wants to do is be a tool, used by the healing hand of God to set you free from sin. And that's just the priest. Jesus has been anticipating the moment you go to confession, whether it's been 2 weeks or 20 years. He wants you to come, seek refuge in him so you can be covered by His loving embrace. He desires a relationship with you and wants you to be happy. He knows, and we know that happiness will only come through the will of God.

Going to confession is like a child running to their mom or dad, confiding in them what's really going on, and receiving love and mercy even though you don't feel you deserve it. Thanks be to God!

Psychologically, confession is healthy for your brain. Many theories in counseling revolve around the idea to take your anxieties, say them out loud, and work through them. This is exactly what happens in confession! It's because God knows exactly what you need, especially in this sacrament. In the confessional, you can claim any sins you've committed, responses to the thought, I'm not good enough, and any times you've doubted God's goodness in you.

I could go on and on about the spiritual reasons to go to Confession, adoration, pray the rosary, etc. However, I am going to focus on why these practices are good for your mental health.

PRACTICE

This week, check out your parish's Reconciliation times. Resolve to go and receive the sacrament. You will be so happy you did!

STRATEGY #13 | ADORATION

RECOMMENDED USE: before, during, and after experiencing anxiety.

Our society has very little silence. There seems to be traffic, sirens, music, social media, kids running amuck everywhere you turn! The way you speak, listen, and comprehend has been under attack due to life's fast pace.

In the article, *Myth and Mystery of Shrinking Attention Span*, Dr. K. R. Subramanian (2018) shed light on the topic. "Communications can be effective only if we allow adequate time for the information to be absorbed; if there is a constant and uninterrupted communication, it may be difficult for our faculties to concentrate sufficiently to absorb what is said." You may not be accustomed to allowing time for processing information. Therefore, you may lose out on the lessons gleaned from reflecting throughout the day. It's common to become overwhelmed and overstimulated as a result.

Know that your brain craves silence because it was created to need silence. Jesus wants you to fully live, being fully present. You must take time in silence to live and love at your full capacity. Thankfully, Jesus gave you a place to sit in that silence:

adoration.   This time with Jesus, sitting in His glorious presence is such a gift! The Church already has a place for you to step outside the world, go to your Creator, and be re-convicted to know you are enough.   Adoration could be compared to the secret ingredient needed for a strong and beautiful mental wellness.

PRACTICE

I challenge you to go to adoration without a list. In adoration, you may try to do all the right things, say the right prayers, and have the perfect disposition. There is no such thing. All you should plan to do is go to adoration and sit with God. That's all He wants. Embrace Him and let Him love you where you're at. This form of silence is powerful and important.

P.S. It is okay if you arrive, slide into your pew, and then notice that your mind is racing, and sitting in silence is hard. But give yourself the gift of time, let God's grace wrap around you as you rest in Him.

P.P.S. If you do not have access to adoration, though it is a tragedy, you can imitate St. Francis by going outside to pray. Find a quiet spot in your backyard, park, or along a trail. Jesus prayed in the desert... think about the silence He experienced while sitting outside just like you.

STRATEGY #14 | ROSARY

RECOMMENDED USE: before, during, and after experiencing anxiety.

The more you learn about mental health, the more you will love the rosary. It is meditative and repetitive. The rhythm of the rosary is soothing like you are resting in the arms of your mother. You repeat the Hail Mary as your mom rocks you back and back, offering peace. This can be hard for some because relationships with mom can be rocky, but Mary is there. She is ready to hold you the way in which you long.

The God who made you, made your brain. He also gave you a connection with His mother. Through the rosary, and asking Mary to intercede for you, she will draw you closer to Jesus, the healer of your soul. Because God created you body and soul, He offers this prayer tool to calm your body, grounding your animal brain in love and safety.

You may ask, what power does the Hail Mary have? Let me show you.

St. Louis DeMontfort said, "The salvation of the whole world began with the Hail Mary. Hence the salvation of each person is also attached to this prayer." When Mary said, "fiat," or, "Thy will be done" she consented to be the Mother of God. Jesus' incarnation, life, and death is possible because of Mary's, yes. Her yes was an act of trust in the will of God, the will to save all of humanity. Your mother, my mother is powerful. She is full of grace and lives as queen mother in heaven. She takes your offerings straight to the ear of her Son. And how can a son refuse his mother?

The rosary is powerful because Mary is powerful. I highly encourage you to pray the rosary, meditating on the mysteries, letting the words imprint on your heart. I recommend finding an audio rosary (found on any streaming platform) because it gives you the choice to pray along, meditate, or just be. It removes any sense of worry; *did I pray it right? Should I say blessed 'are you' or blessed 'art thou' among women? Is this the right order? Did I say ten? Eleven? Six?*

Instead of allowing these thoughts to trample your peace, the audio rosary gives you the gift of following along. You can even use the rosary to help you fall asleep at night. The repetitive nature is akin to having your mother rock you, lull you to a peaceful sleep. St. Bernadette Soubirous said, "In the evening when you go to sleep, hold your beads, doze off reciting them, do like those babies who go to sleep mumbling, 'Mamma! Mamma!'" She holds your worries and fears while you rest. They are safe with her.

PRACTICE

If you struggle to sleep, I have a suggestion. Journal your fears from that day, anything that may be running through your head. (See the benefits of journaling on p. 54) Then, give your fears to Mary. You could have a designated box for her, or a statue on your bedside table. Once the fears are in Mary's hands, play an audio rosary.

WHAT TO DO NEXT?

Your tool belt is now loaded to the brim with strategies. You may prefer some strategies over the others and that's just fine. These tools should help you get off the hamster wheel whether you use one or all fourteen!

These strategies will help you build your house and practicing the tools in your tool belt will build and reinforce your mental wellness. However, you must be sure not to build on sand. Anxiety is one hurdle when building the house, so let's dig a little deeper so you can assess your mental wellness.

STRATEGY #15 | YOUR NET

RECOMMENDED USE: especially before, during, and after experiencing anxiety.

Establish a net of people in your life that you can go to when you are struggling. For some, the use of the net might mean that you are in crisis, and you should absolutely utilize the individuals in your net. For others, this is simply a strategy to assist you in working through difficulties in your mental wellness journey.

Frequently, people look to one person or one thing in their life to be the answer to all their problems. A net isn't made up of one string that would snap under pressure but rather many strings that hold you up. Let's think of this net as a hammock. A hammock has multiple strings that intertwine together that wrap you in support.

To establish this strategy, I invite you to look at all the different people in your life. You're looking for the people who will lovingly wrap you up like a hammock. You might have a friend who is good at problem solving. Or a friend who would love to meet you for dinner. Perhaps a particular friend who likes to watch the same funny movies as you. Work to create this list of all the people in your life who can help you in the various ways that you may need, and who can best support you.

You might have a friend who's really good at listening. If you just need someone to listen, then they'll be able to do it really well. This is a win-win because this person wants your good and wants to help. If when you need a listener you instead go to the "fixer" and ask them to just listen, they're probably not going to do it very well. You likely won't feel heard and they won't feel helpful. This is a lose-lose situation. (Note: sometimes a fixer is what is needed. I often go to my husband and tell him that I need his help as a 'CEO', to help me fix the problems we're facing as a family, and that way he knows that I'm coming to him for that particular assistance.)

I'll use an analogy here - the difference between shooting baskets while blindfolded or shooting baskets with full sight. (Imagine this isn't basketball, but rather a struggle you have in your mental wellness journey.) I'm the person attempting to shoot the baskets and I need someone to be there for me. Most of the time I'm just throwing ball after ball hoping they land somewhere close. Hoping someone out there can love me and support me the way I need.

The idea that causes most people struggles in their anxiety is when someone goes to a potential supporter, but that person isn't set up to help properly, or you're asking something of them that they aren't capable of giving, so then they're hurt that they didn't help and you're sad because you weren't helped. Honestly, most people want to help! It's just that not everybody can help in the same ways. Most people don't use a hammock because in the past they've asked people for things they can't give instead of the things they can. Building your net is about going to the individuals in your life who have intentional strengths so that you can feel confident knowing that you can be supported.

The key is to fight the idea that people don't want or can't help you. People DO want to help and they CAN help you.

How do you go about knowing who you need? Do you need a listener, a fixer, or someone to come over with a pizza who can sit, eat, and just "be" with you? Maybe someone to make you laugh, or someone who will give you a tissue when you need to cry. How do you know? What if you're introverted, or like to stay to yourself? What if you don't feel like you have any friends or family capable of helping? Keep reading!

Make a list of the people in your life; your boss, coworkers, neighbors, family, friends, and ask questions like: *what do I know about them?*, *how have they helped me before?*, *how have I seen them help others in the past?*, *how do they love?*, and ask *what is the method of how they love best so I know what to ask them?* These questions, and this process, are all about intentionality so that you're not throwing the ball up blindly just hoping for the best.

Right now you're thinking "I've talked to these people." "I've tried this already and no one can help me." I know that you have and I know how hard it was, but this time we're going to go back and try it a different way. This different way helps you remove the blindfold so that you can make your shots. The beauty of the net strategy is that we're not putting strain on one person or relationship, we're spreading it out so that you can get the support you need.

"I need nothing but God,
and to lose myself in the
Heart of Jesus."

- St. Margaret Mary Alacoque

CHAPTER 4

ASSESS YOUR MENTAL WELLNESS

CHAPTER 4 | ASSESS YOUR MENTAL WELLNESS

RATIONAL OR IRRATIONAL FEAR

Anxiety is sourced in the fear of not feeling safe. So, let's zero in on the root of the issue, the fear. You must look at the fear of not feeling safe (this fear can be your hole, or it could be fear from past experiences), and determine whether it is a rational or irrational fear. Rational fears are those that deserve the full onset of the fight, flight, or freeze response because you could die, so you need the stress hormones to save you. Irrational fears are those where your life is not in danger, but your thinking brain and animal brain are miscommunicating, which causes the anxiety.

Fearful Situation	Rational Fear	Irrational Fear
Bear attack	✓	
Drowning	✓	
Car accident	✓	
Parent-teacher conference		✓
First day on the job		✓
Proposing		✓

All these fearful situations are legitimate. Remember, rational fears are those where the animal brain and thinking brain agree that death is a possibility. No one is going to die at parent-teacher conferences -- but those can certainly be scary!

It's beneficial to gain awareness of your animal brain's response whether the fear is rational or irrational. Next, you determine whether or not your fear is reasonable.

REASONABLE OR UNREASONABLE FEARS

Reasonable fears are those that are highly likely to occur. Unreasonable fears are those that are extremely unlikely to ever take place.

So, when a fear is identified, take it through the following chart. See where you land.

FEAR FLOWCHART

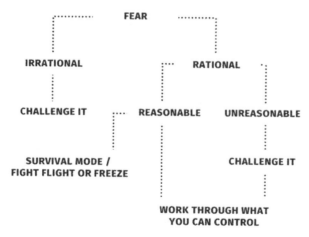

PERSONAL EXAMPLE

I live in the middle of nowhere Kansas where 5 cars pass my house a day. Is it possible I will get hit by a car and die? Yes.

Is it likely? No! So, it seems unreasonable that I would get hit by a car and die. Therefore, I have no reasonable explanation to fear getting hit by a car.

You should only cooperate with the fight, flight, or freeze response when (a) you encounter a rational, fearful situation, and (b) when it is reasonable. If the situation is either irrational, or unreasonable, you need to get off the hamster wheel. The anxiety needs to come to a halt, so the stress hormones cease to enter your body. Most fears are unreasonable. Satan takes sufferings and truths and taints it with falsehood. He tricks you into believing his lies because he embeds little truths into the lie. He uses these lies to create irrational fears in us. But listen, Satan is a liar and thief of joy. Jesus has already defeated him, and Satan runs scared at the name of Jesus.

It's important to know God never leaves your presence. He willed you into existence and his constant love sustains you. Sometimes you will run from him, but He is always waiting for you to return. He longs for you to visit him in the Blessed Sacrament, to shed light on the truths you struggle to see within yourself. Take your fears to the altar and offer them to Jesus, the God who is perfect love.

There is no fear in love, but perfect love drives out all fear.
First Letter of St. John Chapter 4, verse 18

MARRIAGE EXAMPLE

Let's say I have a client who has struggled with marriage.

"It's just never going to happen! I'm never going to find someone, get married, and be happy! It's just never going to happen!"

I would ask, "Is that reasonable to believe? Is there evidence to back this belief?"

The purpose of asking these questions to my client is to understand where the fears are coming from. Are they coming from facts? Or are they stemming from an irrational fear? I take my client through the Fear Flowchart, but you can do this on your own as well.

Taking each step in the flowchart is essential, kind of like going down steps. When you miss one, you stumble down the rest. Your thinking brain needs each step to communicate to your animal brain, for example: there is a fear, and it has a rational component. Only then will you be able to see the fear for what it is, either rational or irrational. Many are unable to discern between rational and irrational because they get caught on the hamster wheel. They may see the fear as irrational, but they lack the skills to challenge the fear. I'm going to say it one more time, you need every step in the process because following each step reveals how you ought to respond to the feelings of anxiety.

The fear of never being married is irrational because the client is not in danger of dying. Let's continue using this example to explore both options, reasonable and unreasonable fear.

EXAMPLE OF A REASONABLE FEAR

My client says, "There are no good guys out there. I don't know how to find anyone."

This is one of the rational fears that we would then acknowledge as a challenge, but then look at how God works in our vocations. We could explore the ways you are open to God's Will in your life. I would ask questions. "Where are you meeting people? What activities are you in? How are you making yourself available to meet a guy with the faith you have and desire in a partner?" We would come up with a plan for what we can do, and we would offer Jesus the aspects we don't have control over.

The anxious response to the fearing single life is irrational, even though the pain is real. When you can see the elements that are real (the fear and sadness), that's when you can use your support systems and tools you've learned to work through the pain. However, idling in the anxious response allows fear to keep you from the freedom you long for. You can see in the following example how Satan takes the truth and twists it.

EXAMPLE OF AN UNREASONABLE FEAR

In this case, the client is a single woman who has never dated. She fears that no one will ever want to spend the rest of their life with her. She thinks she is not pretty enough, smart enough, spiritual enough, etc. She fears that she is destined to be alone. She believes that God has abandoned her and is not listening to her prayer.

Do you see the difference? The reasonable fear comes from evidence, while the unreasonable fear is a baseless fear. I say baseless because the unreasonable fear came from Satan, who took a perverted version of the truth to instill fear. Both situations are difficult, but only one is reasonable, or evidence based.

This information will help you face your fears. And I'm guessing your fears stem from a hole. It's time to see the hole for what it is, and then overcome it.

RECOGNIZE YOUR HOLE

Your holes can be a scary place to go alone. The fears you have, whether reasonable or unreasonable, are real and cause suffering. Most people wait until their house has fallen into the sandy sinkhole several times before seeking help. You don't have to go through the struggle of rebuilding by yourself because Sacred Heart Mental Wellness will be with you every step of the way.

Everyone wants their holes to magically disappear. If I could bottle it up and sell it, I would give Mr. Amazon a run for his money! Instead, it's time to clear the sand so you can see your hole for what it is. So, what is your sand? Maybe you know your sand, maybe you don't. I'll pose some questions to help you start the reflection needed to find your sand. Are you anxious often? Do you struggle with comparison? Is there substance abuse in your life? Is there a disordered desire in your heart? Do you shop to feel better? Do you eat to feel better? Do you hide behind your makeup and clothing?

I present these questions not to be accusatory, but to help you see your sand. Let me repeat: you must see your sand. I need you to do this step (finding your sand) because where your sand lies, your hole is nearby. Resolve to rid yourself of the sand (i.e., go to confession and/or take away the option to use sand), and to never turn to your sand again. You are strong enough to do this! Use the strategies and don't expect to be perfect right off the bat. For the sake of your mental wellness, you must keep trying. Sacred Heart Mental Wellness is with you!

Knowing your sand will almost always help you identify your hole. But if you are unsure of your hole, do some serious reflection on your life. Are there past experiences that impact your day to day living? Is there a regular worry or fear that pops into your mind? What's the hardest thing you have ever been faced with, and did it leave trauma? Is there a situation that puts your mind on the hamster wheel?

Sit with these questions for a while. Allow yourself the time to think and pray about your life. Naming the hole will give you power over it. So, ask yourself those questions now.

As a side note, we all have several holes. I recommend starting with one. Your skills to overcome the holes in your life will get better with each hole you recognize and overcome, so I don't want you to fight all your holes at the same time.

BUILD YOUR BASEMENT

Building your basement is analogous to getting to understand your hole. This includes seeing all the ways your hole has impacted your life. The basement gives structure to the hole, as well as a foundation for the house.

Just like in a construction project, things are going to be a lot messier before they get easier, but they will get better with time and effort.

To start building, you need to understand your hole. Ask yourself questions like it's going out of style. *Why do I think about myself like this? Where did this thought come from? Why did this happen to me? Did I have any control over the situation? Was this situation my fault?* These questions might apply to you, they might not. You know your hole, so you will need to ask the right questions to understand it. Understanding your hole is like laying the concrete foundation for your home. This step is essential for your home to be reliable so take your time with it. Sit in the hurt and allow it to motivate you.

Next, you will need to frame out your basement with 2x4's. This is the part where you take your understanding of the hole and see how it has impacted your life. Remember the example I used about my cousin almost drowning and how I connected it to my experience of lake day? I looked at my "freak out moment" when I couldn't see David Jr. in the water, and asked, *why?*

Connecting the past trauma with the current struggle enlightened me. I was able to explain my response on the pontoon that day as well as my overall hesitancy toward all things water. It was so healing to know why my body sensed danger even though I was safe.

So how do you connect your hole to your current life? I suggest looking at situations that make you uneasy, give you anxiety, or inspire a negative reaction or response. Then, you will take that situation and follow it to its source with my most popular question, *why?*

PERSONAL EXAMPLE

I used to lose my mind when my husband, Dave, grabbed a second beer. Dave is not a small man by any means, nor is he a regular drinker, and two beers were not going to push him over the edge...not even close. But in my mind, two beers were two-too-many, so I would become infuriated.

Why are you drinking? Don't you love me? I can't believe you would do this to our family!

Dave would be so confused. Then he would feel accused (rightly so) and get mad right back! He asked, "Why are you mad? Two beers don't put me in the danger zone. Why are you so upset over a second beer?"

Then I put it together. I was projecting my hole onto my husband. You see, when I was growing up, my dad wouldn't stop drinking after two beers. And two beers meant 6, then 7, then more. My dad has since quit drinking. But I needed to reconcile with my hole: I am the daughter of an alcoholic.

I was able to connect my reality and pain of my hole with my newly-understood response. When you can do this, you'll see how it reduces the power of your hole. Making this connection provides structure to your hole so that keeps the sand out and away from your basement.

Additionally, you will need to bring a mentality of acceptance to the table. No one wants to give up their holes. They are part of what makes you, you. They tell a story about the mountains you've climbed to be who you are today... but you don't want to live in the hole! The hole in your house becomes your basement. There's no need for me, you, or any house guests to go down there. You've accepted the hole yet reinforced your basement with concrete and steel.

The past will no longer define you. The sand and hole shouldn't threaten your house anymore. You will get to choose who you are, and how you are known. For example, I used the neuroplasticity strategy to recognize my past, but change how I understand my identity. Instead of thinking, *I am the daughter of an alcoholic*, I think, *I am Catherine, whose dad was an alcoholic.*

While you do the heavy reflecting, be sure to refer to the strategies provided. These will help you continue with the building process. These will be the insulation and drywall that keep every grain of sand out of your fortified basement.

BUILD YOUR HOUSE

You have identified your hole. You have worked hard to understand it. You have found how your hole impacts your life. Now you need to do something about it.

When I realized and understood the hole I had about drowning, I worked through my options with Dave.

That's when we decided to compromise. I would go out to the lake on "lake day" for two hours. The kids would only swim within my line of sight so I could stay calm. Then, after those two hours passed, Dave would drop me off at the dock so I could go home and enjoy the rest of my Saturday. I restate this solution because this was a huge step toward building my house!

House building is a life-long project, just like your physical health, your mental health will always need "working out" to stay healthy. It helps to have the goal in mind as you build your house, so this is what a house (in progress) might look like.

HOUSE BUILDING

You are fully convicted by the love of God; He loves you and you trust Him. When you have feelings of worry or anxiety, you can see these as natural feelings. You have strategies in your tool belt so you can regain your sense of peace. In conflicts, you can see your contribution to the conflict, understand parts of your past that play a role in how you may have reacted and responded. While recognizing your thoughts and feelings, you see the conflict from the other person's perspective.

You set boundaries for each person in your life because you believe boundaries create life-giving relationships for both yourself and others. You see past life experiences as part of your past, but not defining your future. You understand how your past impacts your current day to day. You use this information to help you make decisions. You move away from caring about other people's opinions because you find your worth in Jesus. It is He whom you strive to please.

Are you there? If you are, you're probably going to be canonized a saint. But for the rest of us, remember that this is the goal. You don't have to be there right now, but hopefully someday you can experience this freedom.

House building takes a lot of work. Even when your house is built, maintenance needs to be done. The strategies provided along with the resources at Sacred Heart Mental Wellness will help you build and maintain your house.

WHEN TO REFER TO A PROFESSIONAL

Mental wellness should be treated like your physical and spiritual wellness. Furthermore, you practice good eating habits and exercise to maintain physical wellness. It's more difficult to start working out if you wait until your physical fitness is in crisis. Similarly, you don't wait for a chasm in your relationship with God before starting to pray. Instead, you pray daily, trusting God in the small things so you are convicted to trust him in the big things.

Therefore, I am so passionate about mental wellness. I have resources ready for you to build up your mental wellness. That said, these tools are not going to be the quick fix you may need in a time of crisis when you are exhausted from rebuilding your house on sand. Think of it like why you don't go to the gym when you're having a heart attack.

Sacred Heart Mental Wellness offers resources to help you before it gets bad, and hopefully prevent the suffering and exhaustion that comes when you don't take care of your mind. I also want to help you gain a better understanding of the people in your life. Anxiety is very common, and it can happen to anyone.

Here are some telltale signs it would be beneficial to see a professional:

+ Symptoms of anxiety or depression are interfering with daily life

+ You experience having trouble getting out of bed

+ You often avoid routine grooming

+ You skip work

+ You experience continuous bouts of crying

+ Conflicts with family members are frequent

+ The house keeps being built, and then falling

Please know that I offer resources for you and that I care. I want you to be the best you that God created. Sometimes, you will need help removing the sand so you can see your hole for what it is. Every good contractor knows that you need the right kind of tools for the variety of challenges life throws at you. Sacred Heart Mental Wellness offers these tools so you can get to building soon and successfully.

"Unless the Lord build the house, they labor in vain that build it."

Psalm 126:1

CHAPTER 5

MENTAL HEALTH IN AND AFTER A PANDEMIC

CHAPTER 5 | MENTAL HEALTH IN AND AFTER A PANDEMIC

I would like to preface this chapter by stating, this is not a conversation about various conflicts associated with the pandemic that began in 2020. I'm describing the pandemic experience as I received it in the counseling office. This is about mental health when your life takes a dramatic shift in a few short days.

As human beings, one thrives on routine. You love what you know, and you know what you love. This is safety. Eating the same cereal for the last ten years is safe. Going to work is safe. Taking your kid to soccer practice is safe. Your animal brain likes your routine because it makes you feel safe.

Now let's look at the beginning of the pandemic. In just a couple of days, everything you once knew and were comforted with was, well...gone.

The conversations being held by the psychologists and counselors of the world began with the struggle: this had not happened in recent memory, and never on such a global platform. Studies have been done in the past where they simulate a quick and unprecedented shut down, but the world has never been so globalized. For the first time in human history, the entire world experienced the same thing at the same time.

THE PANDEMIC EXPERIENCE

Our routines stopped. Therefore, what you identified as safe, also stopped. Do you remember how hard it was to get toilet paper? Especially the brand you preferred.

On a different scale, you were hit by a rational fear of losing loved ones, while being forced to look at the frailty of your life square in the face. You questioned the political agenda surrounding the pandemic, which doubled the stress as havoc descended upon the world. Experimental vaccines sent you into a never-ending search for truth. Fear of your freedom surfaced whether you were on one side of the fence or the other. Riots and protests threatened your safety and stability. On top of it all, the extra time at home opened the door to an increased media consumption. Yikes! No wonder you were anxious!

Before the pandemic, what I witnessed in my counseling office and encountered personally was that people already had a manageable, basic level of anxiety. The onslaught of the pandemic turned everyone's animal brain up a notch. There was a fear that came when you didn't know what the future held. This is the first time in the counseling office where I confirm rational fears frequently. I say, "yes, that is a rational fear. There is a lot you don't know."

MASLOW'S HIERARCHY OF NEEDS

You ought to approach yourself and others with Maslow's Hierarchy of Needs in the back of your mind. Your animal brain is on high alert, so one needs to show compassion. Maslow's Hierarchy of Needs is not perfect, nor meant to be taken as doctrine. However, it is a good reference to aid as you interact with others, and to have compassion on yourself.

Maslow believed that self-actualization was the goal. For you to reach the top of the pyramid, to self-actualize, you must have all the building tiers in order. For the sake of the argument, let's switch "self-actualization" with "being the person God created you to be."

If you become the person God created you to be, you will reach your full potential. St. Catherine of Siena said, "If you become who you are called to be, you will set the world ablaze!" God desires for you to reach your potential, and to have your needs met in the process. You can trust that He will give you what you need when you need it. His idea of your potential and your idea of your potential may not always be aligned. But you have a lifetime to unite your will to the will of God! After all, He wants you to be happy and holy so you can be in communion with him.

Refer to Maslow's Hierarchy of Needs. *(The pandemic knocked out the bottom three tiers.)*

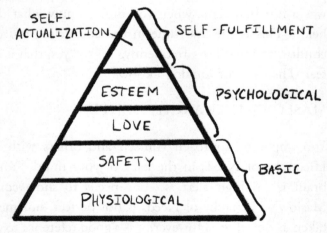

PHYSIOLOGICAL NEEDS

Yes, most had food and water, but there was a rational fear those securities weren't always going to be at my disposal.

Shelves were cleared at the grocery store and there were supply shortages. I remember wanting to buy yeast to make bread but couldn't find any! Even the toilet paper that I always used wasn't available, so I had to find another. The household items that you always used before weren't there, and so our routines and sense of safety went out the window.

SAFETY NEEDS

In the beginning of the pandemic, we didn't have a lot of information. We heard only that it was a virus. It can kill.

It's only natural for your concerns to have gone through the roof. The world desperately looked for information on the most likely victims, how contagious was it going to be, and how did it spread? As a society, we still don't have a lot of the answers to the questions we asked in the beginning.

We all know people who had the virus and breezed through it like they would a mild case of the flu. Additionally, you either know of someone or heard the testimony where the pandemic brought a person to their death bed. Your safety and security had been at risk, and you had to learn how to cope. God did not intend for you to live in a state of fear for sustained periods of time like we saw through the pandemic.

NEEDS FOR BELONGING AND LOVE

When the world was called to keep our distance, we lost connection with our loved ones. Many elderly people didn't get to hug their families for an entire year. In my family, we have Sunday night dinners at my parent's house. Those didn't happen. All these basic interactions were taken away. Zoom video calls replaced the way the world made personal connections. While it was a useful tool, it was not the same as shaking someone's hand, or receiving a kiss from your grandma on the cheek.

When we see the people we care for and can give them a hug, we release the brain hormone serotonin. In an attempt to help people cope with the isolation, we were told virtual was just as good as being in person. But this "feel good" hormone release does not happen through virtual encounters. This may be the reason why many felt disheartened after a virtual meeting with friends.

This caused many people to start on the train of thought we call being on the hamster wheel. People would think there was something wrong with them because the virtual Friday night happy hour did not give them the sense of community that they feel when meeting in person.

GIVE GRACE

Having experienced 2020 and all its turmoil, you must give yourself the grace you need. You are told you should be able to function as well as pre-pandemic while you have cracks in the three bottom tiers of Maslow's Hierarchy of Needs. Grace is realizing that this expectation is not possible right now and that is okay. You only make it worse by being mad at yourself when you are not functioning the same way you used to. For those thinking, "But the pandemic is over. Why is she spending so much time on this?", I would just answer by saying that life is now different and things have changed forever. Just because you aren't as aware of it, trust me when I say that many people, especially those with severe anxiety, are carrying around a huge weight related to the pandemic and the after-effects.

Once we acknowledge the fragility of the bottom three tiers, then we can start using what we do have more effectively.

Each change that pops up has a domino effect of decisions that you need to make. The change to work from home leads to what do I do with the kids? How do I teach them? How am I going to make dinner when I still have work to do? Decision fatigue could also play a part in why the pandemic made you feel the anxious response.

Some things you or loved ones dealt with (or could still be dealing with) are decision fatigue, lack of concentration, not finding things enjoyable that once were, lack of energy, agitation, depression, and anxiety. We are also seeing these feelings become cyclical. Did you think the pandemic was over? Seemingly it is, but as infection numbers rise and fall, more and more people are struggling with pandemic related stress, anxiety, and depression again.

Recognize that your communities are experiencing the same thing on a mental and emotional stage. You must give yourself grace because you are probably not operating at your fullest potential.

The lack of patience and grace is the biggest problem I've seen in counseling. People are mad and disappointed in themselves because they're falling back into their holes. They think they should be fine, but they haven't accounted for the challenges life's thrown at them. Allow me to compare the pandemic experience to a Kansas storm.

TORNADO ANALOGY

In Kansas, we have tornadoes. The weatherman watches the weather patterns, analyzing the data for the public. He checks the forecast several weeks before and sees the trends while remaining aware of the constantly changing theme of weather.

When I am watching the weather updates during a tornado warning (a warning means that a tornado has been spotted and touched down somewhere nearby), I know that at any moment a tornado could come, and I would need to take cover. With that said, most tornado warnings come and go without any imminent danger taking place.

The pandemic was a reminder that sometimes tornadoes come, and we need to be on the lookout but we also can't live our lives in a storm shelter.

EXAMPLE

Since the pandemic, I was asked to interview with EWTN Vatican. The interviewer spoke openly about the creative roadblocks she was facing in preparation for my interview. She said, "how am I supposed to come up with a creative idea if I don't know if I'll be able to get groceries this week? How can I let my mind even focus on work?"

She was right. It's unrealistic to expect her to be creative when her immediate needs for survival are unknown. Again, give grace. Take a deep, grounding breath, and stay close to the sacraments while loving each other through this time.

DON'T WAIT

Your focus on mental health needs to come before or after the crisis. Most of the time, clients wait to see a counselor until the problem is really bad. You must be proactive to cultivate mental health. Waiting to work on your mental health would be like putting your hand in boiling water, then calling your doctor, waiting on hold, and finally speaking to your doctor only to have him say, "Take your hand out!"

Hopefully, you were taking steps to work on your mental health before the pandemic. But if you weren't, there's no time to begin like the present! Professionals see the ramifications of the pandemic on mental health. Whether you realize it or not, the pandemic turned your animal brain up a couple notches. This part of your brain was focused on survival during the pandemic, which resulted in a hole. Using the strategies provided, you will learn how to get off the hamster wheel as pandemic memories are triggered.

Sacred Heart Mental Wellness has resources ready to guide you in the cultivation of your mental wellness. Don't wait to use the strategies in preparation for feelings of anxiety. And don't wait to reflect on your hole so that you can overcome it sooner rather than later. Sacred Heart Mental Wellness offers the tools, and now it's time to build your house!

"One must not think that a person who is suffering is not praying. He is offering up his sufferings to God, and many a time he is praying much more than one who goes away by himself and meditates his head off, and, if he has squeezed out a few tears, thinks that is prayer."

- St. Teresa of Avila

CHAPTER 6

THE STEPS

CHAPTER 6 | THE STEPS

An area that I often see people get stuck in overcoming their anxiety and emotions is when they try to skip the proper steps. They need to validate their feelings, work through their feelings, and then take actions to manage their feelings. Many times they would rather skip these important steps and hope that they can land safely at the bottom, but that very rarely happens. If we take this analogy more literally, we could think about going down a flight of stairs. Stairs built in the United States are required to be a certain width and depth so that when someone goes down the stairs, they know exactly how to go down them. Our brains know the distance because of muscle memory, and we can typically go downstairs without even thinking about it. But what happens when someone accidentally misses a step? No matter how hard they try, if a step is missed, they stumble and fall.

When working with clients, this is often the same pattern I see, just with emotions instead of a set of stairs. If we don't want to fall at the bottom of the stairs, we need to look at what each of the steps look like so that we can know that we are stepping on each tread. Please let me clarify, many people have struggled with this analogy because they are so afraid of getting stuck on a certain step that they just try to skip them all together. I am not saying that we need to stay on one step for a very long time, but we need to stay on the step for enough time to acknowledge that the step exists and to prepare ourselves for the next step that we're about to take.

Let's work to make this a little bit more clear. When our animal brain senses fear, the initial step that we need to do is acknowledge our fear. Acknowledge that it is normal for the animal brain to assess dangers and that it is simply trying to take care of us. Once we have done this step, then we can go to the next step, but not before.

Step two is trying to better understand the fear or the anxious response that has occurred. *Is this a rational or irrational fear? Is it likely or unlikely to actually happen?*

The third step is to gain a better understanding of the stimulus of the anxious response that is happening, asking *"if it is rational or irrational, why is that?"*

Step four is to take action - either rejecting an irrational fear or an unlikely chance of something happening, or working to come up with a plan if it is a rational, reasonable fear so that we can work through the challenges.

Step five is to be encouraged with yourself for taking all five steps and coming safely to the bottom of the stairs. (Even consider being thrilled and excited for yourself!) This is a very important step that is so often ignored or forgotten.

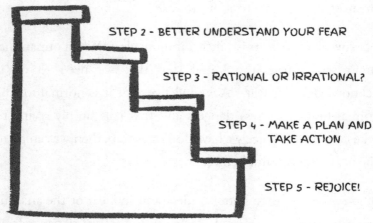

STEP 1 - ACKNOWLEDGE YOUR FEAR

STEP 2 - BETTER UNDERSTAND YOUR FEAR

STEP 3 - RATIONAL OR IRRATIONAL?

STEP 4 - MAKE A PLAN AND TAKE ACTION

STEP 5 - REJOICE!

Whenever we are trying to retrain the brain into a new neuropathway, we have to encourage that pathway. Our brain needs positive reinforcement to continue the good (and often difficult) behavior. So, whenever we get to the bottom of the stairs, we need to take a moment to make it concrete in our mind and in our body, that we have taken these steps and have come to an ending that has kept us safe. This will help a brain want to go through this process again the next time we have an anxious response. Also over time, the more we do these steps and have positive outcomes, the anxious response will become less exaggerated, because the animal brain will know that there is a plan to handle an anxious response.

To look at this in a more practical way let's take a story from the Bible and go through the steps with it. The story that I think is very impactful for people struggling with anxiety is the story where twelve year old Jesus is found by His parents in the temple.

Step 1: Acknowledge - In the Finding of the Child Jesus in the Temple (*see The Gospel of St. Luke, Chapter 2, verses 41-52*), we see Mary and Joseph going through the step of first acknowledging that they fear that Jesus is missing. (*Be clear - this was not a sinful fear.*) They must acknowledge that there is fear and what the fear is about before they can do any of the following steps. If Mary had skipped this step, it may have gone something like this: Mary talking to herself, saying, *"I'm not sure where Jesus is, but I'm sure he's with Joseph. I'm sure he's fine. I'm just going to ignore this feeling in my gut. Everything is okay. I'm just not going to talk to Joseph about this."* That would not have been good. Instead, Mary took the first step and acknowledged the feelings that she felt in her heart and talked to Joseph to see if he knew where Jesus was.

Step 2: Better understand the fear - In this situation, Mary was able to go to Joseph and ask him if he knew where Jesus was, and when they both realized that neither of them knew His location, they understood that they had a problem. Coming to an understanding sets them up for the next step, which is asking, is this a rational or irrational fear?

Step 3: Rational or Irrational? - In the story, we know that Jesus wasn't with them, for He was in the temple. His unknown whereabouts and wellbeing was in question at the time, and that was a rational fear of the parents that left Him behind. This is when Mary and Joseph knew that they needed to go back and find Jesus.

During this step we should talk about some of the irrational fears that one may be experiencing while also dealing with rational fears simultaneously. The fear that I always think about during this story was wondering whether Mary questioned if Jesus was okay? To me, that's a challenging question because He is God and the Son of God and she knew this fully. Mary knew that God the Father had a plan for His life and so in that moment, though she may be worried rationally where He was and how she was going to be able to find Him, there is also possibly an irrational fear of wondering if He was safe. Mary knew that God was protecting Him, and she could reject that irrational fear.

Having fear [I am describing the type of fear that is a sorrow] is not a sin. (The topic of fear is widely debated, which we are not doing here, but Mary was sinless and still had sorrowful fears.) Imagine how you would feel if you lost your child.

Step three is the place where we decide what we do with our fear. Do we give our fear (rational or irrational) to God or do we keep them from Him? God wants to walk in the fears with you and to help you to see the goodness and the love in His will. Part of step three is being able to give him the fears that sometimes we are ashamed of, embarrassed by, feel guilty for, or especially the ones that seem too difficult to give over to Him.

Step 4: Make a Plan & Take Action - In the story, we see Mary and Joseph heading back to Jerusalem to find Jesus. They retraced their steps, stuck to the plan to find Him, and they did. The fear and worry about what may have happened to Him did not get in the way of executing their plan. They knew that they had to go and find Jesus - it was as simple as that. As parents, sometimes there are things you simply must do. I bet they feverishly retraced their steps, asked people if they'd seen Him, and so on. Those were all tangible, concrete steps that they could take to help find their son.

When we have irrational thoughts, we have to be able to reject them in this step, being able to say "No! This is not a rational thought. I reject it, and give it to God." When you are able to reject irrational fears, you are much more likely to be able to execute the plan.

Step 5: Rejoice! - You've made it down the stairs, and haven't fallen. Be thrilled for yourself! Rejoice in the finding of Jesus! Mary and Joseph were relieved, excited, and most of all, grateful that Jesus was alright.

Step five is where we celebrate having gone through the (difficult) steps. Mary and Joseph went through each step one by one. In the end, they were with Jesus and able to rejoice in finding Him. Earlier, you imagined what it would be like to have a missing child. Can you also imagine what the story would be like if Mary hadn't done these steps? She would have had a much different outcome. Be like Mary - do the steps!

Once I've reached the bottom, I always like to thank God for walking down the steps with me and for the grace and encouragement to take each step one at a time.

"Everything that comes
from the
Sacred Heart of Jesus
is sweet.

— St. Margaret Mary Alacoque

APPENDIX

PRAYERS TO THE SACRED HEART OF JESUS

PRAYERS TO THE SACRED HEART OF JESUS

O, Most Sacred Heart of Jesus, I place all my trust in Thee.
(Say 3 times slowly. This is a good prayer for a communion meditation or prayed to help slow your heart rate or control your breathing.)

O Jesus, through the Immaculate Heart of Mary, I offer you all my prayers, works, joys, and sufferings of this day, for all the intentions of your Sacred Heart, in union with the Holy Sacrifice of the Mass throughout the world, in reparation for my sins, for the intentions of all my relatives and friends. Amen.

Lord Jesus let my heart never rest until it finds You, who are its center, its love, and its happiness. By the wound in Your heart pardon the sins that I have committed whether out of malice or out of evil desires. Place my weak heart in Your own divine Heart, continually under Your protection and guidance, so that I may persevere in doing good and in fleeing evil until my last breath. Amen. - St. Margaret Mary Alacoque

From the depth of my nothingness, I prostrate myself before Thee, O Most Sacred, Divine, and Adorable Heart of Jesus, to pay Thee all the homage of love, praise, and adoration in my power. Amen. - St. Margaret Mary Alacoque

Most Sacred Heart of Jesus, pour down Your blessings abundantly on Your Holy Church, on the Supreme Pontiff, and on all the clergy. Grant perseverance to the just, convert sinners, enlighten infidels, bless our parents, friends, and benefactors, assist the dying, free the souls in purgatory, and extend over all hearts the sweet empire of Your love. Amen. - Indulgence of 300 days, once a day - Pope Pius X

O Most Holy Heart of Jesus, fountain of every blessing, I adore You, I love You, and with lively sorrow for my sins I offer You this poor heart of mine. Make me humble, patient, pure, and wholly obedient to Your will. Grant, good Jesus, that I may live in You and for You. Protect me in the midst of danger. Comfort me in my afflictions. Give me health of body, assistance in my temporal needs, Your blessing on all that I do, and the grace of a holy death. Amen.

O Most Holy Heart of Jesus, fountain of every blessing, I adore you, I love you, and with a lively sorrow for my sins I offer you this poor heart of mine. Make me humble, patient, pure, and wholly obedient to your will. Grant, good Jesus, that I may live in you and for you. Protect me in the midst of danger; comfort me in my afflictions; give me health of body, assistance in my temporal needs, your blessings on all that I do, and the grace of a holy death. Within your Heart I place my every care. In every need let me come to you with humble trust saying, Heart of Jesus, help me. Amen.

Litany of the Sacred Heart of Jesus

V. Lord, have mercy on us.

R. Christ, have mercy on us.

V. Lord, have mercy on us. Christ, hear us.

R. Christ, graciously hear us.

V. God the Father of heaven, have mercy on us.

God the Son, Redeemer of the world, have mercy on us.

God the Holy Spirit, have mercy on us.

Holy Trinity, one God, have mercy on us.

Heart of Jesus, Son of the eternal Father, have mercy on us.

Heart of Jesus, formed by the Holy Spirit in the Virgin Mother's womb...

Heart of Jesus, substantially united to the Word of God...

Heart of Jesus, of infinite majesty...

Heart of Jesus, holy temple of God...

Heart of Jesus, tabernacle of the Most High...

Heart of Jesus, house of God and gate of heaven...

Heart of Jesus, glowing furnace of charity...

Heart of Jesus, vessel of justice and love...

Heart of Jesus, full of goodness and love...

Heart of Jesus, abyss of all virtues...

Heart of Jesus, most worthy of all praise...

Heart of Jesus, King and center of all hearts...

Heart of Jesus, in whom are all the treasures of wisdom and knowledge...

Heart of Jesus, in whom dwells all the fullness of the Godhead...

Heart of Jesus, in whom the Father was well pleased...

Heart of Jesus, of whose fullness we have all received...

Heart of Jesus, desire of the everlasting hills...

Heart of Jesus, patient and rich in mercy...

Heart of Jesus, rich to all who call upon you...

Heart of Jesus, fount of life and holiness...

Heart of Jesus, propitiation for our offense...
Heart of Jesus, overwhelmed with reproaches...
Heart of Jesus, bruised for our iniquities...
Heart of Jesus, obedient even unto death...
Heart of Jesus, pierced with a lance...
Heart of Jesus, source of all consolation...
Heart of Jesus, our life and resurrection...
Heart of Jesus, our peace and reconciliation...
Heart of Jesus, victim for our sins...
Heart of Jesus, salvation of those who hope in you...
Heart of Jesus, hope of those who die in you...
Heart of Jesus, delight of all saints...
V. Lamb of God, who takest away the sins of the world,
R. Spare us, O Lord.
V. Lamb of God, who takest away the sins of the world,
R. Graciously hear us, O Lord.
V. Lamb of God, who takest away the sins of the world,
R. Have mercy on us.
V. Jesus, meek and humble of heart,
R. Make our hearts like unto thine.
Let us pray: Almighty and eternal God, look upon the heart of thy most beloved Son and upon the praises and satisfaction which he offers thee in the name of sinners; and to those who implore thy mercy, in thy great goodness, grant forgiveness in the name of the same Jesus Christ, thy Son, who livest and reignest with thee forever and ever. Amen.

Heart of Jesus, I give my heart to Thee; but so enclose it in Thee that it may never be separated from Thee. Heart of Jesus, I am all Thine; but take care of my promise so that I may be able to put it in practice even unto the complete sacrifice of my life. Amen.

Blessed Miguel Pro

Memorare to The Sacred Heart of Jesus

Remember, O most kind Jesus, that none who have had recourse to Your Sacred Heart, implored its assistance, or called for mercy, have ever been abandoned. Filled, and animated by this same confidence, O divine Heart, Ruler of all hearts, I fly to You, and oppressed beneath the weight of my sins, I prostrate myself before You. Despise not Your unworthy child, but grant me, I pray, an entrance into Your Sacred Heart. Sustain me in all my combats and be with me now, and at all times, but especially in the hour of my death. O gracious Jesus! O amiable Jesus! O loving Jesus! Amen.

"We the Christians are the True Israel which springs from Christ, for we are carved out of His Heart as from a rock.

-St. Justin Martyr

REFERENCES

Bishops' Committee of the Confraternity of Christian Doctrine. (2010). The New American Bible: Revised Edition. Our Sunday Visitor.

Catechism of the Catholic Church. Vatican City: Libreria Editrice Vaticana. p.362. (1994)

Did you know Pope John Paul II asked us to return to the Prayer to Saint Michael? (2017, January 30). Aleteia. Retrieved August 21, 2021, from https://aleteia.org/2017/01/30/did-you-know-that-pope-john-paul-ii-asked -us-to-return-of-the-prayer-to-saint-michael/

Subramanian, Dr. K.R. (2018) Myth and Mystery of Shrinking Attention Span. International Journal of Trend in Research and Development, 5(3), 2. http://www.ijtrd.com/papers/IJTRD16531.pdf

The Marian Room. (2018, August 17). St. Bernadette and Childlike Trust. The Marian Room. https://www.themarianroom.com/st-bernadette-and-childlike-trust/

RESOURCES

It would be impossible to give you years' worth of counseling advice in one single book (at least not one that anyone would read). I've compiled a list of resources for you to continue your mental health journey. Our homes always need work and Sacred Heart Mental Wellness has the right tools!

SacreHeartMentalWellness.com. Visit to find resources to cultivate mental wellness. Note: the resources on our website are updated and change - please return to the site frequently.

> **Mental Wellness Assessment:** Take this short, FREE assessment to receive a real-time description of where you are on your mental wellness journey. When you know where you are, you're better able to move forward.

> **Understanding Mental Wellness Introductory Webinar:** A short and easily digestible instructional video, on the basics of mental wellness. Discuss the key components to mental wellness and how being proficient in these areas helps you in your everyday life.

> **"The Biology of Anxiety from a Catholic Perspective" Video:** A 30-minute introduction video that will aid in the Catholic's pursuit of mental wellness by providing you an overview of your brain and God's beautiful plan for you. This video looks at your brain's role in anxiety, and the common reasons why people fall into anxiety and remain there.

> **Book Catherine:** Catherine travels the world speaking, running retreats, and training clergy/teachers/first-responders/staff, etc. To book her, visit the site to contact us or email:
>
> info@SacredHeartMentalWellness.com

"Confession is a Place of Victory" on YouTube. Fr. Mike Schmitz discusses the glory of the Sacrament of Reconciliation. Search the title above, or https://youtu.be/YiVjwlUO9Sc?si=BjqB1UvgDBw_7oUT.

"Do not let the past
disturb you - just leave
everything in the
Sacred Heart
and begin again
with joy.

-St. Teresa of Calcutta

ABOUT THE AUTHOR

Catherine DiNuzzo, MA is a Licensed Professional Counselor in private practice, who also operates Sacred Heart Mental Wellness. Catherine utilizes traditional cognitive-behavioral counseling practices all through a Catholic lens. Catherine is faithful to the Magisterium and operates her practice in that same manner.

She has compiled her many years of counseling experiences and style into digestible, tangible, and easy-to-consume online resources for the Catholic who wants to live a mentally fit lifestyle. Catherine hopes that Sacred Heart Mental Wellness can help provide you with easy-to-use tools and techniques to achieve mental wellness in your life.

Catherine earned her Master's Degree in Counseling and Human Services from the University of Colorado-Colorado Springs. Prior to her private practice, Catherine worked for several years in both schools and in agency counseling, namely with Veterans and services such as Veterans Upward Bound and Vet Centers, working with PTSD. Catherine specializes in helping clients to overcome anxiety and depression, as well as other concerns. She has spoken internationally on the topics of mental wellness, as well as for FOCUS, EWTN, EWTN-Vatican, EWTN-Ireland, The Military Council of Catholic Women, numerous Catholic radio stations, and more.

Catherine and her husband, Dave, live in a small rural town in the middle of Kansas with their four amazing children.

O, Most Sacred Heart of Jesus,
I place all my trust in Thee.

Made in the USA
Las Vegas, NV
17 June 2024

91147044R00075